REFRAME

HOW TO CHANGE YOUR CONVERSATIONS TO RESOLVE THOSE MESSY CONFLICTS

YVONNE DOUMA

Reframe: How to Change Your Conversations to Resolve Those Messy Conflicts

www.doumaleadership.ca

ISBN: 978-1-77277-425-2

References to internet websites (URLs) were accurate at the time of writing. Authors and the publishers are not responsible for URLs that may have expired or changed since the manuscript was prepared.

Limits of Liability and Disclaimer of Warranty

The author and publisher shall not be liable for your misuse of the enclosed material. This book is strictly for informational and educational purposes only.

Warning - Disclaimer

The purpose of this book is to educate and entertain. The author and/or publisher do not guarantee that anyone following these techniques, suggestions, tips, ideas, or strategies will become successful. The author and/or publisher shall have neither liability nor responsibility to anyone with respect to any loss or damage caused, or alleged to be caused, directly or indirectly by the information contained in this book.

Medical Disclaimer

The medical or health information in this book is provided as an information resource only, and is not to be used or relied on for any diagnostic or treatment purposes. This information is not intended to be patient education, does not create any patient-physician relationship, and should not be used as a substitute for professional diagnosis and treatment.

Publisher
10-10-10 Publishing
Markham, ON
Canada

Printed in Canada and the United States of America

DEDICATION

I dedicate this book to my family.

First, my immediate family, **Fritz**, my husband; **Ben** and **Nicole**; **Alicia** and **Harold**; **Jessica** and **Jason**; **Alexandra** and **Fred**; and **Taylor** and **Aiden**. And to all of my grandchildren, who I love deeply. Please know conflict is okay if done right. This book may be able to help you in hard times. This is my legacy to you.

Second, to my extended family: **Mom**, **Dad**, **Harry**, **Joe**, **Ed**, **Glen** and your awesome families. I dedicate this to you and hope it may help in a small way to resolve those messy conflicts.

Thank you all for encouraging me to follow my dreams.

Loving you always,
Yvonne

TABLE OF CONTENTS

FOREWORD

Have you ever had to deal with "Negative Nancys" who cause you nothing but stress and aggravation? If the answer is yes, you don't have to worry. What Yvonne Douma has written in this book is life-changing.

Yvonne provides you with the tools you need to have difficult conversations with even the most challenging people!

Reframe is full of research-backed strategies and practical, easy-to-implement techniques for resolving conflict. It also teaches you how to deal with bullies and aggressive people.

Yvonne shares her expertise in communication and conflict management in a way that enables you to take bite-sized chunks of learning.

Yvonne presents challenges and benefits. She demonstrates how to view a conflict from different perspectives. She teaches the importance of taking ownership. And she provides you with tools to identify the situation and grow your "communication chops" to prevent conflicts from escalating.

Yvonne's authentic teaching process shows you how to gain control over your relationships. By recognizing variables which go into what causes conflict, you can identify triggers and have the tools to calm down and easily resolve situations.

You will be able to identify yourself in the stories and real-life examples shared in this book. And you will learn the necessary skills to have difficult conversations to nurture your relationships.

This book provides you with the technical know-how and the pragmatic knowledge to make real, sustainable changes in your relationships.

If you are a woman in business, who struggles with workplace relationships, this book is a MUST-READ, as it will teach you how to take on a leadership role when resolving conflict.

Moreover, you will stop doubting yourself and learn to *believe in yourself* again! And from the confidence you will gain, you will learn to *love yourself* again!

If you are experiencing conflict in your life, this book is an essential tool kit.

If you want to advance in your job and have a happier life, this book is the golden ticket and will take you there!

Raymond Aaron
New York Times Bestselling Author

ACKNOWLEDGMENTS

Of course, I thank my awesome family for their love and support during the time I decided to write a book! They have been the best encouragers. Thank you, Fritz, for going along with my crazy ideas and supporting me in them; thank you, Ben, for always believing in me and being on my side; thank you, Alicia, for letting me work things out with you, and for being there when I need you; and Jess, you are the most common sense of them all! Thank you for being such a calming presence in my life. Alex, even in the midst of all your own hardships, you always had time to come and cheer me up when I needed it; and Taylor, you have grown into such an amazing person. You have always been interested in what I am up to, and are quick to come for a quick coffee if I need motivation.

A huge thank you to the incredible people you have married: Nicole, Harold, Jason, Fred, and Aiden. You have all been supportive of my career and new endeavours. I could not have asked for better sons and daughters-in-law!

Thank you, Mom and Dad. You have believed in me since I was a little girl, encouraging me to live my life in love, integrity and truth. Even now, in your elderly years, you continue to love and support me.

Thank you to my brother, Joe, for being such an advocate of mine. From a very young age, you believed in me. You encouraged me. You motivated me. You have always been excited about my career and now recently, the book I was going to write. It took a while, but it is done. You will definitely get a signed copy!

Thank you, Kevin and Kandy, for the last 13 years of friendship. Even though you may not have known I was writing a book until the last few months, you have been beyond my friends throughout these years—you have been my family, being there through good times and bad times.

In addition, I have had many other family friends over my life: Nick and Wendy, Pim and Margreet, Cathy, and Shannon, to name a few. You all played a piece in this book because of the many conflicts we have all had at various times in our lives. We talked, we shared, and we resolved so many things together. Perfect research!

David Williams – He was my peer, mentor, and coach, and always believed I could do more than I ever believed I could. He passed away 10 years ago, but I can still hear him say, "Just do one thing, and then another, and your dreams will become a reality!" To this day, I use this saying.

Jonathan Michael – He also is my cheerleader, challenging me to do what I do not want to do. His coaching helped me be able to coach others.

Patricia Ross – Thank you so much for the encouragement and friendship you have given me in the last 5 years at GroYourBiz. You have been an inspiration to me, and your support through the good and bad times was so appreciated.

Speaking of GroYourBiz, ladies, thank you so much. Like Patricia, you have inspired me and strengthened me, and have pushed me to keep on going. You have been so precious to me.

Doris Woodman McMillan – You have been a friend, client, peer, and fellow Rotarian, and I thank you for being there. We have been through a lot together. And to all my fellow Rotarians, it is incredible who God puts in your life at the right time. I have noticed this time and time again.

To my clients, who have helped in the research of this book…

thank you. It has been an honour to serve you, and I hope this book will help you deal with conflict in a healthier way.

I cannot forget to include the Raymond Aaron team, who were instrumental in getting this book to its completion. They helped me with making my words flow (Christine), and with editing, formatting, the creative book cover, and publishing. It has been an incredible journey.

Recently, I have been working with Susan, from Evision Media. She has pushed me to do things I honestly did not want to do. Thank you, Susan!

In addition to the above, there are many others who have inspired and motivated me along this journey. You know who you are and I thank you for being you.

Throughout my life, I have been wrapped in the tender, loving hands of my Saviour, Jesus Christ. He has guided me to where I am now. I had many blessings and many challenges in my life. They prepared me for who I am today. I am blessed beyond measure.

INTRODUCTION

You've been told a lie.

Girls don't have to be "passive" to get ahead at work.

Women make incredible leaders. But they need the communication skills to ascend to higher positions. Women need to call people out on their "BS" when they are not acting like team players. However, this needs to be done in a way that does not completely crush them.

Hmmm. But this may be difficult for you, as you've been conditioned to play nice and take what's given to you. It's a girl thing.

But I'm telling you, you need to be assertive. To get ahead, you need to have the skills and confidence to guide discussions that are going-off-the-rails.

Otherwise, women like you will remain stuck in menial positions where they feel unappreciated and, at times, disrespected.

I know what it's like to put your heart and soul into your job, only to feel like you are not recognized. And what's worse is having to watch the "company jerk" get all of the recognition and promotions.

You deserve better.

Wouldn't it be great if you could leave work at the end of the day feeling like you were a contributing member of the team?

What would it feel like if you worked with people who were kind and respectful to each other? Doesn't that sound lovely?

Well, it is completely possible. I mean it!

You need to learn how to have difficult conversations. I'm not talking about destructive conversations, which are toxic and painful. I'm talking about having the know-how to lead a conversation with someone, which allows you to have a win-win outcome.

Doesn't that sound amazing?

I promise you, it's possible for you!

While I have written this book with women in the workplace in mind, this book will be an excellent choice for just about anyone. Consider this book your personal communication and conflict resolution tool kit. It will show you how to be an authority on building relationships—even with people who are difficult to get along with. Yes, even the team jerk.

This book will teach you all about conflict: what causes it and how to mitigate it. You'll learn the necessary skills to improve your emotional intelligence so you can navigate relationships. You'll also learn about different communication styles, including how to deal with passive-aggressive and aggressive (angry) people. You'll know how to recognize your own triggers and keep yourself calm during conflict. And you'll know what words to say (and not say) during a conflict.

Seriously, learning these tools will be priceless and truly transformative.

You will feel like a queen of communication and conflict when you are done reading this book!

How do I know this? I've spent the past 20 years training women just like you on how to be effective leaders, with kick-butt conflict management and communication skills.

I wrote this book for YOU because I wanted to help you grow your career.

I know how important it is to maintain relationships in the

workplace, and how crucial they are for putting you in a role that will get you promoted.

Knowing how to communicate and relate with people is undoubtedly the most important skill-set you need to develop, especially if you want to advance in your career. By learning how to avoid triggers and stay calm, you will resolve conflicts in a way that makes you feel in control.

Knowing how to navigate your relationships will improve your ability to focus at work. And by taking the leadership role to demonstrate what healthy workplace communication looks like, you will shine like the diamond you are.

I dare you to read this book from cover to cover.

Then, I dare you to do the exercises and answer all the questions.

I dare you to reflect on yourself and your relationships, and see similarities in the scenarios and examples provided. Then I dare you to journal on it.

Next, I dare you NOT to be a fabulous communicator.

I dare you NOT to become the leader you were born to be!

I dare you.

NOTE

I want to hear from you! After getting promoted to the job of your dreams, contact me to let me know how this book enabled you to step into your power!

CHAPTER ONE

CONFLICT? WHAT CONFLICT?

"People fail to get along because they fear each other; they fear each other because they don't know each other; they don't know each other because they have not communicated with each other."

– Martin Luther King Jr.

Congratulations on taking a step towards understanding how to effectively manage communications and conflict so you can ultimately rock your relationships!

In this first chapter, we will be looking at what conflict is, what your personal ownership (for creating or contributing to negative conflict) is, how your relationship history (including past trauma) impacts your ability to cope with conflict effectively, and how to have intentional communication that is a win-win for everyone!

How has conflict in your life been treating you? Do you cringe at the thought of talking to someone about something not easy to talk about? Do you retreat when conflict happens, or do you react with anger? Do you deny something you did, or do you apologize when it is brought up to you?

For some people, the word *conflict* brings up fear and bad memories; and for others, it's just another day at the office.

However, it's quite common to experience conflict in our relationships—sometimes with people on the street or out in public.

ARE YOU OFTEN UPSET BY OTHERS?

- Do you have problems with colleagues who make you upset, but you never tell them?
- Do you feel devalued by your boss?
- Are you too afraid to say something because you think you'll be fired?
- Does your best friend often hurt you with her mean comments?
- Are you upset when your spouse frequently comes home late from work?
- Do you go over conversations in your head, which gives physical discomfort (e.g., headache, stomachache)?
- Are you afraid of confronting someone because of their possible reaction?

If so, this book is for YOU!

Societal conflicts—which occur due to class, race, cultural hierarchy, religion, politics, and land ownership—can become quite scary, as they often, but not always, escalate into protests, riots, violence, and even war. Some of these ugly conflicts reared their ugly face across America in 2020 and continued into 2021.

I could go on and on about the conflicts facing this world today; however, we are going to be focusing on interpersonal conflict.

Whether at work or home, we can reframe our conversations to prevent and mitigate those ugly conflicts from happening.

WHY CONFLICT HAPPENS

Human psychology is fascinating. What makes humans tick and what gets us upset varies significantly from person to person. Even within the same families, there can be many conflicts between siblings, parents and children, and couples.

When we communicate with someone, there is *always* an opportunity for the conversation to go sideways. People often find themselves in arguments with loved ones when it was *not* their intention. So, while not intending to be hurtful is important, what we say and how we say it is what counts, as our words matter.

What I mean is, you may not intend to hurt your friend's feelings, but because you were rushed for time or stressed out about money, you flipped out on them and were cruel in your delivery. The result is you caused harm to the relationship.

If you care about the person, it's up to you to fix what you broke, which means owning up to what you said, apologizing, and doing better the next time.

But then there are times you say something you think is harmless, and conflict still occurs. The reason this happens is we all have different filters. It can be confusing because what you say can be upsetting to one person and okay for someone else. It's because we are all so different.

As we each walk through the world, we view it through a different lens. Based on who we are and our life experiences, we inevitably view situations differently because of our lens or filters.

WHAT DO YOU BRING TO A RELATIONSHIP?

We have acquired ways of thinking, feeling, and acting, based on the bits and pieces we picked up along our journey. The bits and pieces (often referred to as "baggage" or "stuff") are what make us who we are. It is what differentiates us from others. It is what makes us unique. And it is what makes us flawed.

Much of your bits and pieces are made up of the following:

- Your life experiences/how you were raised
- Your values and beliefs
- Communication and interpersonal skills
- Needs, wants, and goals
- Perceptions and attitudes
- Cognitive distortions
- Broken (past) relationship "baggage"/broken heart/ protective walls
- Pressures/stress/fears/power
- Trauma or abuse
- Self-awareness/personal development

What we do with our bits and pieces and how well we communicate with others is due primarily to our emotional intelligence (EQ)—we will discuss this in Chapter two. A higher EQ enables us to understand ourselves, manage our emotions, relieve our own stress, overcome challenges, read people's signals, empathize, communicate effectively, and defuse conflict. In other words, we can *play nicely* with others in the sandbox!

In addition to the above list of bits and pieces, our personal concepts can impact how well we get along.

If you are in a relationship, have you looked at the differences or similarities between you and your partner?

WHAT ARE YOUR CONCEPTS OF MONEY?

- What are your habits—are you a saver or a spender?
- Are you a risky or conservative investor?
- Do you run up your credit cards and pay only the monthly minimum, or pay off the entire amount when the bill comes in?

If you and your partner differ on these, there is plenty of room for conflict to occur.

WHAT IS YOUR CONCEPT OF RELATIONSHIPS?

- Do you have traditional gender roles, or do you prefer a modern approach?
- Do you want to have children, or do you prefer to borrow your sister's kids when you get the urge?
- What are your thoughts on disciplining children?

How much you and your partner differ on these concepts will likely determine how many repeat arguments you have.

WHAT ARE YOUR CONCEPTS OF WORKPLACE COMMUNICATION?

- Do you write general emails, or do you write them according to the audience (e.g., peer, supervisor, client)?
- When an idea is raised in a meeting, do you discuss your objection to it then and there, or do you prefer to talk negatively behind your colleague's back?
- If your officemate talks too loudly during their phone calls, do you say something rude or politely ask them to be mindful of their volume?

WHAT IS CONFLICT?

Conflict is not a bad word. Often, we avoid conflict in our society because we do not want to make the other person angry. This leads to group-think: "Everyone agrees so we can keep the peace." This is especially a trait Canadians have. What we need to realize, though, is if we have a differing opinion, this can add to the idea already on the floor. And then ideas can build.

Let's establish what conflict is. According to Vocabulary.com, a conflict is a struggle or an opposition. If you and your best friend both fall in love with the same person, you will have to find some way to resolve the conflict. Conflict comes from the Latin word for striking, but it isn't always violent. Conflict can arise from opposing ideas.

As people are incredibly diverse, there are many opportunities for conflict to occur in our lives. Even though conflict can sometimes be challenging to get through, we need it in order to grow and thrive. Yes, you read correctly. We need to work through conflict with others to become better versions of ourselves.

One of my favourite verses is from Proverbs (27:17), which tells us, "As iron sharpens iron, so one person sharpens another."[1] It is so very true; if you simply stand back and let the iron stay in a clump, what good would that do for everyone?

WHAT IS YOUR CONCEPT OF CONFLICT?

- When your partner is upset with you, do you run for the hills? Or do you prefer to tackle the conversation as soon as possible?
- Are there specific rules of engagement (behaviour) that are acceptable for you? Does your conflict often include hurtful language?

[1] https://www.biblegateway.com/passage/?search=Proverbs%2027:17&version=NIV

- Do you need to resolve conflict before bedtime, or are you content with going to sleep angry?
- When you are angry, do you resort to name-calling or the silent treatment? Or is a type of behaviour a deal-breaker for you?
- Do you believe conflict is normal and a great way to work things out? Or do you believe conflict is unhealthy, and so you avoid it at all costs?
- Do you see workplace conflicts (among your peers) as opportunities to contribute to dysfunctional gossip so you can get close to the popular crowd?
- How about when you get into a conflict with a colleague? Do you immediately run to their supervisor to complain or try to work it out first?

PEOPLE WHO CONFLICT WELL TOGETHER, STAY TOGETHER!

How couples resolve conflict is a strong indicator of how successful their relationship will be. Why? Disagreements can help bring couples closer together; addressing issues, solving them, and letting them go afterward helps build a tight bond. It allows you to know and trust each other more. And when you do it right, you can learn from your conflicts so you don't repeat the same communication mistakes over and over again.

Then there are the relationships we have with family members, friends, neighbours, colleagues, and acquaintances, presenting unique opportunities for conflict and learning. Therefore, it's just as important for you to use effective communication in *all* of your relationships.

Conflict is not something to run and hide from. Instead, it's an opportunity to have healthy and helpful communication to resolve immediate differences and improve relationships. When done correctly, resolving conflict allows you the chance to state your point of view and say how you feel.

COMMUNICATION TOOLS ARE YOUR FRIEND

When you disagree with someone, your automatic response may be to react and act based on how you feel about the conversation. But, *how* you handle it varies greatly. It's essential to identify what is happening in the situation and be aware of your internal resources (communication skills) *before* you start to react.

You will learn specific tools and skills that will become part of your "Communication Toolkit" later in this book. As communication hiccups and conflicts arise, you can draw on these tools to help resolve many miscommunication situations you may find yourself in. What's more, you will be able to handle communication with more ease and less pain, preventing any verbal hiccups from occurring, based on your newfound knowledge!

Ultimately, with all communication, you can choose to be positive (e.g., respectful, kind, helpful, understanding). Alternatively, you can choose to have the situation escalate into something more serious by being negative (e.g., sarcastic, hurtful, judgmental, mean-spirited).

HOW TO AVOID STICKY CONFLICTS

Situational awareness is crucial for helping you to resolve conflict. An example of this is knowing what you and the other person bring to the relationship, as well as any other issues that may increase stress and anxiety in either of you.

Reading body language is vital. It's best not to attempt any serious conversation when you can see your partner is upset about something. Unless you have a zen-like effect on your partner, allow them time to calm down. In the meantime, you can offer support.

As you can see, timing is also very significant. After all, you wouldn't want to attempt a serious discussion on parenting style while your partner is glued to the television watching a *Super Bowl* Game! Nor would you ask your boss for a raise when she is up to her eyeballs in quarterly reports. Or would you? This is not a communication-friendly environment, so it's best to wait for a time when you have your partner's attention.

Sensitive issues such as addiction or abuse need to be handled with the utmost care due to their inherent nature to create explosive or painful conflict. It's best to seek support from a trained third party on how to broach particularly difficult subject matter so you don't cause harm to your partner or to your relationship.

MAKING SENSE OF EVERYTHING AND RELATING TO OTHERS

People have an innate desire to be meaning-making machines. Have you ever noticed you have to make sense of everything to feel safe, understood, respected, etc.? It's part of our human nature. We need to not only attach meaning to everything, but we also make up stories to make sense of what we see, hear, and experience. For example, if we are treated poorly as a child, we grow up believing there is something wrong with us. Our story is we are unworthy or unlovable. The problem with carrying these negative stories throughout our lives is it becomes facts in our minds, impacting our thinking and actions, and ultimately damaging or destroying our relationships. It's always best to work through this type of inner conflict you are experiencing, so as not to contaminate your relationships. Not to mention hinder your goals.

We also feel the need to put things, and especially people, into boxes. We have difficulty processing the complexity and uniqueness of individuals, so we categorize them into proverbial boxes. For example, kids are often put into boxes such as athletes, musicians, and geeks. As we grow older, we continue with this type of categorization. I'm sure you have heard of the expression helicopter mom, soccer mom, wine mom, blogger mom, or career mom. There are comparable boxes for men that I won't mention, as I suspect you get the point.

Knowing we tend to use boxes to help us relate to others, are you aware of any boxes you may have been put into by your "friends" or colleagues? Is it possible you have put yourself in a box and it inhibits your ability to communicate with people?

KEEPING OUR BRAIN CALM DURING CONFLICT

It's important to stay calm during conflict. Harvard Business Review suggests four steps to calm your brain and manage yourself during conflict:[2]

- **Stay Present:** be aware if you are feeling provoked, by noticing your body cues. Have a visual cue such as your happy place (e.g., a place or a person that makes you feel good when you think about it).
- **Let Go of the Story:** even if you feel threatened, try to let go of your thinking or judging mind, as it often fills up with stories and thoughts about what is happening at the moment.
- **Focus on the Body:** be open to focusing on sensations in your body–even if they are uncomfortable.
- **Finally, Breathe:** breathe rhythmically using the same number of counts for the exhale as your inhale (e.g., inhale 1-2-3-4, hold 1-2-3-4, exhale 1-2-3-4 (or longer if you can). Science tells us deep breathing can change our physiology. For example, it slows down our heart rate and calms our brain, allowing us to focus. So before walking into a stressful situation, take ten deep breaths and visualize you are breathing in confidence and

---

[2] https://hbr.org/2015/12/calming-your-brain-during-conflict

success with every inhalation. With every exhalation, you are breathing out fear and anxiety.

HOW PAST TRAUMA IMPACTS OUR ABILITY TO MANAGE CONFLICT

You may not be aware, but the reason you struggle to communicate effectively and resolve conflicts could be because of any trauma you experienced in your life. The long-term effects trauma has on your ability to communicate and resolve conflict can be mild to severe—depending on how much "inner work" you have done on yourself.

Trauma does not only involve rape, molestation, child abuse, and murder. It can also include family violence, divorce, loss of loved ones, car accidents, dog attacks, workplace injuries, life-threatening illnesses, political violence, and war. It can be less obvious things such as emotional abuse and being told you are a loser or will never amount to anything. I have personal experience with people close to me who still suffer from those words they received as a child. Words hurt. Words matter. And when these words are used later by someone else, they are triggered, and go back to the feelings they had as a child.

Trauma is all too prevalent in our society. The Canadian Psychological Association says, "76% of Canadians report having experienced a traumatic event during their lifetime."[3] Not surprisingly, the National Council for Behavioural Health says, "70% of adults in the U.S. have experienced some type of traumatic event at least once in their lives."[4] There is a trend in North America. However, I suspect it is more of a global phenomenon.

---

[3] https://cpa.ca/sections/traumaticstress/simplefacts/

[4] www.thenationalcouncil.org

Trauma is all about pain. And because trauma can be so devastating, conflict and criticism can often feel like:

- You are being judged
- You are being attacked
- You are being dismissed
- You are weak, like a victim
- You are unloved or unworthy

Even for the most "evolved" person who has spent years doing inner work (e.g., therapy, self-help, self-love), everyday communication can be triggering and upsetting. Add some underlying trauma, and you have a recipe for more pain and conflict.

Any new conflict is often experienced as a new trauma for anyone who has experienced trauma (or a new wound). To make matters worse, the new trauma is being stacked on top of the old trauma that still lives inside you! It's no wonder you feel upset or get defensive when some type of miscommunication occurs. Receiving any type of criticism must be incredibly difficult for you because you feel like you are under attack.

Some people might refer to your old trauma as "emotional baggage," which can understandably make you feel bad about yourself. I prefer to use less harsh expressions, such as "stuff" or "bits and pieces," as I've referred to earlier in this chapter. The important thing is to choose words that work for you, which do not cause others pain.

So, you experienced trauma in your life; how you feel now is not wrong or right—it just is. You spent a lifetime overcoming stuff that was outside your control. And it sucks to be able to deal with some of the long-term effects of the trauma.

Whatever happened to you, know you are *not* damaged goods or broken. You are *not* less than or unworthy. But there is essential work that needs to be done to feel like you are *whole* or *healed*.

Why would you want to engage in personal inner work that will cause you pain? Doing your inner work allows you the chance to work through your stuff so you can become the best version of yourself. You get to do this for YOU—and no one else.

WHAT'S THE ALTERNATIVE?

Walking through the world with unresolved trauma causes us to see ourselves as victims, and others as perpetrators. We are often in reactive mode, frequently triggered by what other people do or say to us. It's because the pain is hiding beneath the surface.

This presents in different ways. For example, we can retreat and feel like a powerless doormat. Think about it. If your life is full of bullies and perpetrators you blame for your pain, you may want to look at what's going on inside. Find your voice. Find support. And work on you!

Alternatively, you can go through your life lashing out at others. But this is no way to live life! It will destroy your relationships and, possibly, career opportunities. You may become a bully. No one likes bullies. You may feel justified in freaking out. Consider people in your life may have been caught in your crosshairs (because they said the wrong thing or said something the wrong way). If you continuously get into conflicts and horrible arguments with others, you could become defensive (due to the pain) and feel the need to fight back. Or you may be a "right-fighter," someone who obsessively feels the need to be right.

Then there are the lucky few who built the courage to invest in themselves. You did a ton of inner work, and you feel strong. You may feel like you are a pretty good communicator. Great! But because we can't control how other people act or speak, there is a good chance you will still become triggered and find yourself in an ugly conflict. No worries! I will be covering this a bit later in the book.

Did you know trauma is stored not only in our mind but also in our body (cells and tissues) and our spirit? Talk-therapy alone cannot heal you. It's often helpful to do some wellness activities such as walking, running, yoga, and tai chi, as they also enable a strong mind-body connection.

If you are interested in trying some alternative therapies, you could look into Rapid Eye Therapy, otherwise known as Eye Movement Desensitization and Reprocessing (EMDR), as it was originally designed to alleviate the distress associated with traumatic memories.

You could also look into energetic work (e.g., Reiki, healing touch, and therapeutic touch) to release the trauma from your body, mind, and spirit.

Regardless of where you find yourself, this book will help you identify the best way to respond during a conflict so you can resolve it peacefully and amicably for both of you. You will learn new tools to reframe your conversations, strengthening your relationships. You will no longer seek victory or defeat but rather work towards gaining a mutual understanding and a win-win outcome.

ARE YOU MOTIVATED TO OWN YOUR PART?

I believe people need to be 100% willing to own their stuff. It takes two people to *make* or *break* a relationship. If we all own our own parts, it will be much easier to work through our issues and resolve our conflicts.

To this end, you will need to learn new skills. This book will help you express yourself in ways to benefit relationships by communicating more effectively and resolving conflict by reframing your conversations.

We cannot control the behaviour of others. We can merely communicate our needs and wants, and hope they comply. Because it takes two people to make a relationship work, it is essential to ask yourself what you are doing to contribute to the relationship.

First, you need to do some of the crucial inner work to be the *best version of yourself.* With audiobooks and podcasts, it's never been easier to learn and develop ourselves. Are you ready to look at yourself and be honest and identify where you are coming from?

Second, you must put a conscious effort into being the *best colleague you can be.* Hmmm, what does that look like?

We all go through life, often feeling like we know what's best for our relationships. But do we? Are you ready to own your part in the success and failure of your relationships?

Are we mirroring dysfunctional behaviours we learned from our parents? Do we have massive self-esteem issues we need to work through to avoid becoming a doormat for our partners?

SIMPLE WAYS TO BE LIKED IN THE WORKPLACE

The following list may give you some ideas on how to improve workplace relationships:

1. Become a person who does at least one nice thing each day.
2. Don't pretend to be anyone else; be you.
3. Aim for a win-win outcome instead of trying to be right.
4. Be respectful and pay attention to your colleagues.
5. Don't expect your boss to be your best friend or parent.
6. Support the vision and mission of your company.
7. Demonstrate leadership and solid communication skills.
8. Be empathetic towards colleagues.
9. Do inner work on yourself.
10. Learn to respond after taking some time to process what's happened.
11. Keep an open mind when discussing the situation.

12. Be considerate and kind to others.
13. Be patient with people.
14. Learn to say, “Tell me more.”
15. Listen instead of thinking about what you want to say next.
16. Communicate with your ears (listen more; talk less).
17. Remember, you are either contributing or contaminating relationships.

INTENTIONAL COMMUNICATION

It’s essential to understand the basics of what it’s like to be intentional with your communication:

1. Think before you speak. Be mindful of what you say, how you say it, when you say it, and why you say it.
2. Be aware of your body language (e.g., facial expression, tone, posture, body movements) controlled by your subconscious mind.
3. Be sensitive to the state of the person with whom you are communicating (e.g., are they in a bad mood?).
4. Know your listener and choose your words to speak their language (e.g., formal, informal, casual).
5. Be aware of how you feel when you communicate. Do you have a pattern of communicating when you are upset? If so, wait until you are calm.
6. Understand your communication style (e.g., aggressive, passive-aggressive, submissive, manipulative, assertive).
7. Choose the appropriate communication channel (e.g., non-verbal, such as email, text, direct messaging, social media, in person face-to-face, by phone, by video).

IT'S NOT YOU; IT'S ME

Be honest with yourself, and be prepared to accept responsibility for your part in what happens, especially when there is a communication breakdown.

I get it's difficult right now with everything going on in the world. Even our government representatives can't seem to get it right.

But it's not all about you, you, you. It's about "us" and "we." It is not "either/or"; it is "both/and." We need to be mindful of what is happening to the other person if we want to communicate effectively. For example, just because you had a rough day at the office does not permit you to snap at your family when you get home. You don't know what type of day they had.

Put on your big girl or boy pants and become responsible for the energy you create in your environment. If you want to live in a healthy, loving, and peaceful home, you need to be healthy, loving, and peaceful in your communication with others!

In other words, *be at cause* in your relationships.

And be careful to pick your battles!

"If we could change ourselves, the tendencies in the world would also change. As a man changes his own nature, so does the attitude of the world change towards him."

– Mahatma Gandhi

IN CONCLUSION

In this chapter, we looked at what you bring to a relationship, including the bits and pieces from your past and what your concept of successful communication is. We talked about why it's essential to take responsibility and how intentional communication fosters successful relationships. In the next chapter, we'll take a deeper dive into who you are and why you communicate the way you do, as we look at emotional intelligence (EQ).

REFRAME WHAT YOU NOW KNOW

You are *not* a victim of circumstances. When relationship communication breaks down, it's because both parties (yes, you!) contributed to the breakdown.

Do you recognize situations in your life where you may have contributed to the breakdown in communication?

Taking ownership is the first step in solving the problem. It is not about self-blame and making you feel bad. But instead, it should help you recognize situations where your "messy bits," concepts of conflict, and past trauma may be contributing factors as to when you find yourself in conflict.

The goal is to identify areas where you can reframe your communication, and implement what you have learned. This book will have plenty of opportunities for you to reflect on what's happening for you.

REFLECTIONS

What came up for you in this chapter?

What did you learn about yourself?

What was your biggest takeaway?

What surprised you most?

Which area do you need to work on most?

What do you plan to change?

What's your first step?

Which tools will you use to improve your skills?

CHAPTER TWO

WHO ARE YOU?

"I think self-awareness is probably the most important thing towards being a champion."

– Billy Jean King

In this chapter, we will be discussing who you are so you can understand and manage yourself, which will enable you to understand better and be aware of others and manage your relationships with greater ease.

WHO ARE YOU?

To answer this question would require profound reflection on your part. After all, you are a complex, living, breathing human being. You are the composite of characteristics, beliefs, and values that make up your personality and behavioural patterns. Within your social relationships, you are often defined by the roles you play, such as parent, child, sibling, friend, colleague, and neighbour. And in civil society, you are considered an individual with rights and responsibilities.

And then there is how you see yourself. Your thoughts and feelings about who you are and how you present to the world help define yourself.

Some people might say how successful you are in life is who you are. But only you can define what success is for you. It is not your desires and how hard you work that determines your success in life; it is what you *believe* to be true about yourself that determines your ability to make serious changes and achieve your dreams.

EMOTIONAL INTELLIGENCE (EI)

As you can see, defining a person is quite intricate. So, for now, we will focus on one key area: emotional intelligence (EI), which includes:

- **Self-awareness** – being cognizant and able to understand your own strengths, challenges, and emotions
- **Self-management** – being able to control your own emotions by using restraint, composure, or self-mastery
- **Social awareness** (managing social relationships) – being aware of others and your surroundings and being able to influence others emotions through verbal and non-verbal communication and interpersonal skills
- **Relationship management** (awareness of others) – being able to understand and discern other people's emotions (and being able to share their feelings)

SELF-AWARENESS

In Chapter one, we touched on the need to be self-aware and how we need to have a high EI to manage conflict effectively.

Just as participants in twelve-step programs need first to recognize they have a problem; you will need to identify your communication issues and behavioural habits. By utilizing self-awareness, you will be able to work on any problems needed to be addressed.

Since you want to improve your communication and conflict skills, you will need to first recognize your current strengths and weaknesses in this area. Not only this but what your body language and tone of voice adds to your communication. It is also necessary to consider your interpersonal and social perspectives (your interactions in social settings). All of this requires self-awareness.

It may be uncomfortable to look within and take an inventory of things you do not feel good about. However, self-awareness is critical, as a high EI will enable you to identify your emotions and triggers. More importantly, it will help you become aware when they occur, allowing you to manage the effects in real-time, preventing your triggers from having a devastating impact on your life.

By improving your self-awareness, you will be able to identify your emotions as they first arise. If you are the type of person who flips out (yells and screams) at people when you get upset, becoming in tune with your emotions will provide you with emotional freedom. You will not feel like your emotions are hijacking your body and mind whenever you get upset. Being able to control your temper to have effective communications with the people in your life will undoubtedly be appreciated most by those around you.

Self-awareness requires you to become aware of your personality, habits, likes, dislikes, needs, behaviours, goals, strengths, successes, and failures. More on this will be covered later in this chapter. Knowing what makes you tick and lights you up will help you to navigate while engaging in social circles and workplaces.

One of the ways you can do this is to become aware of physical sensations in your body. Mindfulness meditation or being present (in silence) with what you are experiencing will enable you to recognize better when bodily sensations are trying to get your attention.

Being cognitive of situations and people who typically upset you can help you anticipate your upcoming emotional reactions, giving you more control over the situation.

As we talked about trauma and triggers in the previous chapter, I thought it necessary to review some of the internal triggers you may experience during conflict situations. As you become aware of the internal triggers, you can mitigate their effects, allowing you to maintain control over your responses.

INTERNAL TRIGGERS

- Physical sensations such as rapid heartbeat, sweaty hands, or spinning head
- Pain or tense muscles or the sensation to run, freeze, or hide
- Extreme headaches
- Being aware of overwhelming emotions such as anger, sadness, and anxiety
- Uncomfortable feelings such as feeling vulnerable, afraid, helpless, or out of control
- Seeing, hearing, smelling, or tasting things tied to your original trauma
- Feeling overwhelmed, vulnerable, abandoned, or out of control

SELF-MANAGEMENT

Having a sense of self-management and self-control in your personal life is just as important as it is in your work life.

While self-management in the workplace enables you to contribute to a healthy and productive work environment for you and your colleagues, it also allows you to have healthy and satisfying relationships with the people in your personal life.

Moreover, as people are social creatures, maintaining our relationships is necessary for our joy and happiness. Many of the skills we employ at work, such as patience, perception, resilience, and regulating our emotions, are necessary to build and sustain meaningful relationships.

Self-management also means taking responsibility and ownership for your own actions and doing your best to contribute positively to relationships. It means organizing your thoughts and your time to focus on what is truly important.

Self-management skills are essential in the workplace because they help you contribute to a better work environment for yourself and your coworkers. However, they can also carry over into your personal life. Examples of self-management skills include self-confidence, persistence, resilience, patience, perceptiveness, and emotional regulation.

To this end, you need to be aware of your weaknesses and triggers to regulate your emotions and stay in control—even in situations that are way outside your control. Remember, you cannot control others, but you can control how you react to what happens in your life.

When people are triggered, a fascinating sequencing of events takes place that causes our brains to, in a sense, shut down. This impairment makes it difficult to respond to situations as our best selves.

Therefore, it's best to come up with a plan so you can anticipate your natural reaction and choose a response where you are in control of what you do or say.

Being mindful and present, no matter if you are at work or home, will enable you to pick up on your body signals telling you that you are getting triggered so you can do some self-talk (in your head) to remind yourself where you are right now, and some grounding techniques (to stay calm).

HEALTHY STRESS RESPONSE TO USE AT WORK – CLIENT EXAMPLE

One of my clients, Debbie, was hired to build relationships in her role. Unfortunately, her boss was fired a year later, and the new boss who came in did not value relationships like her previous boss. The new boss completely changed the position and requirements even though Debbie had no training or knowledge in that specific area. It impacted her ability to communicate, and her confidence was shaken. Although her new boss's aggressive language and lack of emotion often triggered Debbie, she did her best to stay grounded and composed. Debbie was proud of her ability to remain professional when all she wanted to do was climb under her desk and hide. When she got home from work each day, Debbie made it a point to do some self-care, as she knew the constant stress was taking a toll on her body, mind, and soul. Long story short, Debbie was fired a short time later because she wasn't meeting the expectations. But because Debbie was self-aware of her talents and boundaries, she could anticipate what was happening. As such, the job loss did not come as a complete shock to her.

What's more, she took care of herself during the stressful process, getting her rest, talking to family and friends, and eating healthy. This change could have been so much more devastating had Debbie not been as self-aware as she was. She managed the outcome marvelously and soon found a new career she was perfect for. Debbie was mentally prepared for the change, so it was not as devastating as it would have been.

Think about what Debbie had to endure. She was no longer qualified for her job (due to the changes her new boss implemented). Debbie had to deal with male aggression and a significant personality change, which made her feel unsure. She felt disappointed and increasingly doubtful of her ability to succeed in her new role. But she knew her strengths and could remind herself she had excellent interpersonal skills, which were reflected in the fact she was a great "people person." Debbie knew her talents would be valuable in a new company, as she was a great communicator and teacher. She was ready to move on.

This situation demonstrates how using grounding techniques helps you remain calm to communicate with others clearly and effectively. If you find yourself in a panic and triggered state, it would be impossible for you to be a helpful colleague. Therefore, using self-care resources is key to helping you maintain your relationships.

TECHNIQUES TO USE WHEN YOU BECOME TRIGGERED

Being triggered and going through a trauma response takes a toll on us. Afterwards, self-care is super important, as working through conflict can be scary. If you become triggered, there are strategies you can implement to provide yourself with some relief.

- **Practice relaxation techniques** (deep breathing, meditation, grounding exercises, aromatherapy, music, affirmations, visualizing your happy place)
- **Call someone if you are feeling triggered** (have a list of people you can call whenever you need them for support)
- **Keep a journal** (helps you to process your feelings and recognize which situations are triggering for you)
- **Become aware of your triggers** (be mindful and write down what situations or people tend to trigger you)

- **Anticipate and plan a coping strategy for triggers** (as you become more self-aware, you will be able to anticipate your triggers better)
- **Exercise regularly** (helps to reduce stress)

PREVENTION IS KEY!

Being able to deal with conflict and manage yourself effectively will help you maintain control in your life, helping save your relationships and your job.

I would be remiss if I didn't mention the importance of prevention, which means planning.

If you accept stress and conflict will occur at home and work, you can plan for it. This means learning grounding techniques, practicing self-care routines, and having some conflict resources and hacks that help you stay in control and not bring attention to yourself while you are doing it.

Take time to prepare a list of conflict resources:

- **Grounding techniques** (to help you remain present)
- **Relaxation techniques** (to stay calm)
- **People you can call** (your best friend or therapist)
- **Tools you can use** (e.g., rescue remedy)
- **Skills you could learn** (e.g., public speaking, assertiveness training)

Sometimes just knowing you have options will help you to remain calm.

Many things in life can be enormously stressful, even if you have never experienced trauma. Some examples include public speaking, job interviews, swimming with sharks, jumping out of planes, and swimming with dolphins.

Since most of us have had to experience the stress of preparing for and enduring a job interview, I wanted to give you an example of coping with stressful emotions.

First, being self-aware of who you are and all you have to offer the company is key to winning them over. To that end, you need to keep your emotions (and stress level) in check.

Of course, you can implement these techniques anytime you are about to engage in a difficult conversation.

"Surround yourself only with people who are going to lift you higher."

– Oprah Winfrey

SOCIAL AWARENESS

Social awareness means being aware of the people around you.

For example, if you have a conversation with someone, do you pick up on their changing body language? Do they suddenly cross their arms (defensive stance), have an annoyed expression on their face, grind their teeth, exhale loudly, or tap their foot? These are all signs something is up. Something you are saying is annoying them. Or it could be they are late for a meeting or an appointment and don't have time to talk to you. Pick up on their cues and ask if you are keeping them from something. This will allow them to end the conversation to help mitigate their distress.

How are you when approaching a new group of people? As you enter the room, what are you looking at? Do the people look upbeat and happy, or is the mood solemn or serious? How about at the dog park? What are the dog owners talking about? Can you join in the conversation and add some value?

Regardless of the type of group or event, when immersing yourself in the group and the setting, you may want to make sure your body language is neutral or matching theirs. Body language is nonverbal communication, including facial expressions, posture, gestures, eye movements, sense of space, and touch. The thing is, body language is often subconscious. You do not know you are doing it.

If you enter a meeting where everyone is joking and laughing, you know this will be a light, fun interaction, and you can join in the fun so you can mirror the behaviour. However, if you notice most people have negative or defensive body language after reading the room, and you can feel the tension in the air, be mindful it will be a sensitive environment, so be careful with your words and how you present yourself. You are a happy person. Continue to be kind and considerate. Do not change the awesomeness you are.

The recipe for success is to look for cues, be aware of others, and manage yourself.

If you are sensitive to energy and have picked up on the negative body language of a select few, it's best to position yourself away from them. Instead, seat yourself next to the people whose energy naturally matches yours.

One of my clients, Jackie, recently attended an event to network. It was meant to be a fun social gathering, and she was looking forward to it. She was going alone, but she was not worried, as she loved meeting new people. When she arrived, only a few people were there. She began introducing herself to others in her usual friendly manner. As she went from group to group, she started to realize most of the people she had met there were quite negative; talking about politics, COVID-19, bashing school teachers, discussing profit of banks, and talking about their bosses.

The body language was closed, and their tone of voice was ridiculing. Jackie began to feel super uncomfortable. When they started asking her what she did, she suddenly felt small. She loved her career and felt she added much value; however, she was definitely on a different playing field with these women. She began to be triggered by a memory of another meeting she attended where similar things happened. Her heart was beating fast, she had sweaty palms, and her head was pounding. Jackie knew she had to get out of there. She left soon after. This was not a suitable environment for her. By the time Jackie reached home, she was in a bad mood and went to bed.

Body language and tone of voice make up 93% of all communication. And as you can see from this example, being around negative people starts to affect your health. Thankfully, Jackie figured it out sooner rather than later.

RELATIONSHIP MANAGEMENT

To manage your relationships with others, it all starts with you. You need to be on point with your self-awareness and self-management to be conscious of how others perceive you.

It's also important to read other people so you can get a sense of their mood and how open they might be to a difficult conversation or sharing of any kind.

Understand everyone is unique. Even if you have eight kids, chances are they will all have differences in their personalities. It's important to recognize and celebrate those differences in others rather than try to make them change who they are. Everyone doesn't have to be like you! They need to accept and treat you with respect.

Many arguments start because people assume what the other person is thinking. Or they assume what the intention was of the other person based on their behaviour. It's best to inquire as to why someone did or said something to you that was hurtful rather than freak out on them for nothing.

Be aware of your attitude (positive or negative) and how you present yourself affect the people around you.

Sometimes taking a few deep breaths can help you calm down, stopping you from saying something you may regret later on.

Think of your relationships as precious cargo that needs to

be nurtured. You can't throw it around and expect it to like you afterwards.

If you join a group of friends or colleagues who are all laughing and telling jokes, it wouldn't be the time to be "Debbie Downer." If you are upset about something, it is much better to have a one-on-one conversation with someone you trust.

Some techniques will enable you to create a thriving environment, helping you maintain relationships with friends.

QUICK TIPS FOR MAINTAINING POSITIVE RELATIONSHIPS

- Communicate and compromise with each other. Also, provide positive feedback and reassurance to each other.
- If you have a conflict, seek a fresh perspective from a third party, as they may help you see the situation from a new light or advise on how to resolve the conflict.
- Conflict is best resolved with cool heads. Take some space apart to allow time for you both to look at the situation from both sides. And prepare what you want to say.
- Agree to disagree. We don't have to have the same beliefs or opinions. But we do need to respect the other person's right to theirs.
- As the family unit is important, try your best to solve problems with them. Chances are, their disapproval is based on their concern for you because they love you. Keep this in mind, as they are not the enemy because they disagree with your choices.

NOW THAT YOU KNOW WHAT EI IS, WHAT DO YOU NEED TO WORK ON?

THE BIRKMAN METHOD – PERSONALITY ASSESSMENT

As EI is a strong determinant for how well a new employee will fit into the existing workplace culture, many employers do personality and EI testing on prospects before hiring them. I use the Birkman Method, as it uses positive psychology to assess personality.

This assessment is one of the finest assessments I have used in my leadership experience. So what is it?

The Birkman Method® began in 1951. Called the Test of Social Comprehension, creator Dr. Roger W. Birkman developed this test following his experiences in the war, where he recognized that pilot performances and learning were greatly impacted by the visual and interpersonal perceptions of the pilots. Today, the Birkman Method® has been used by millions of people worldwide to help them gain insight into their motivations, perceptions, and human behaviours. It is used by thousands of companies worldwide to help employers understand prospective and current employers better. The tests help determine how someone is likely to behave and what their motivations are.

Birkman's method collects data in four key areas:

Motivation, Self-Perception, Social Perception, and Mindset.

MOTIVATION

As motivation influences how we feel about the work we do and how well we do it, Birkman's method measures passion and interests in the workplace. The data measures broad interest themes, which are typical of workplace roles and initiatives.

SELF-PERCEPTION

Our perceptions of ourselves impact how we present ourselves (show up) to the world. This data point reveals how we feel about managing relationships, giving back to our community, and performing everyday tasks. Our feelings are often based on the styles we have assumed in the past that have netted us positive results.

SOCIAL PERCEPTION

We process information using our internal filters to determine if we feel comfortable in certain situations or environments. How we feel internally dramatically impacts how we act or react when changes occur. Knowing our needs and expectations helps us to anticipate our reactions and avoid having stressful behaviour.

MINDSET

As our mindset impacts how we deal with interpersonal, intrapersonal, and work alignment issues, it's essential to recognize our perspective to understand what is driving us to think and behave in a certain way (from a conscious and subconscious level). This part of the assessment gets to the roots of our belief systems.

Why do I, along with thousands of other businesses, use it? Employees with a high EI are more aware of and able to control and express their emotions professionally. What's more, having a high EI is a strong indicator the new employee will blend into the organization's corporate culture, as they will be more aware of their colleagues' emotions, which can help foster better working relationships.

I have used the Birkman Assessment for hundreds of clients, and it is the most accurate assessment I have used. Once I go over the assessment report with my client, I ask them a fundamental question: "How close is this to reality for you?"

Without a doubt, I have yet to receive less than 90%. This is incredible. As Birkman has hundreds of different uses through different reports, phrasing things in different ways allows my clients to say, "Yes, this about sums it up." Birkman is not necessarily a feel-good assessment. The clients I use it with realize that reality, and sometimes the truth, hits them in the face. In short, it identifies your usual behaviour, which everyone sees; your needs to stand in your strengths, which no one sees; and your stress behaviours.

If you would like to learn more about the Birkman Method, visit https://www.doumaleadership.ca/birkman-method-canada/. If you are interested in taking the assessment, please reach out to me (my contact information is at the end of Chapter ten), as I am a certified consultant at Birkman International Inc.

EI'S 4 DOMAINS AND 12 COMPETENCIES

There are many emotional intelligence models, each with its own set of abilities; they are often lumped together as Emotional Quotient (EQ) in the popular vernacular. Daniel Goleman prefers "EI," which defines as compromising four domains: self-awareness, self-management, social awareness, and relationship management.

EI is more than knowing ourselves, being aware of others, and being kind and respectful and sensitive to others' needs. Within the four domains, there are 12 EI learnable skills and competencies that enable high performing employees to work as a leader and model ideal behaviour for the organization.

These areas include emotional self-awareness, emotional self-control, adaptability, achievement orientation, positive outlook, empathy, organizational awareness, influence, coach and mentor, conflict management, teamwork, and inspirational leadership.

SELF-AWARENESS	SELF-MANAGEMENT	SOCIAL AWARENESS	RELATIONSHIP MANAGEMENT
Emotional self-awareness	Emotional self-control	Empathy	Influence
	Adaptability	Organizational awareness	Coach and mentor
	Achievement orientation		Conflict management
	Positive outlook		Teamwork
			Inspirational leadership

Figure 1. Emotional Intelligence Domains and Competencies, by Goleman, D. & Boyatzis, R.E. 2017. Reprinted and retrieved from https://hbr-org.cdn.ampproject.org/c/s/hbr.org/amp/2017/02/emotional-intelligence-has-12-elements-which-do-you-need-to-work-on. Copyright 2017 by Goleman and Boyatzis.

EI NEEDED FOR OUTSTANDING LEADERSHIP

Recent neuroscience studies demonstrate that when we can focus in three different ways, leaders can manage their companies while developing strategies and fostering innovation.

"Every leader needs to cultivate this triad of awareness, in abundance and the proper balance, because a failure to focus inward leaves you rudderless, a failure to focus on others renders you clueless, and a failure to focus outward may leave you blindsided."

Therefore, using a combination of all three by focusing on yourself (self-awareness and self-control); focusing on others (using cognitive empathy, emotional empathy, and empathic concern), building relationships; focusing on the wider world (strategy and innovation); and then putting it all together, will help position you as a leader of leaders![5]

---

[5] https://hbr-org.cdn.ampproject.org/c/s/hbr.org/amp/2013/12/the-focused-leader

"Self-awareness is one of the rarest of human commodities. I don't mean self-consciousness where you are limiting and evaluating yourself. I mean, being aware of your own patterns. I think self-awareness is probably the most important thing towards being a champion."

– Tony Robbins

IN CONCLUSION

In this chapter, we looked at Emotional Intelligence. EI is genuinely fascinating because when we are in tune with what makes us tick, we can be better versions of ourselves. When we understand our motivations, perceptions, and mindset, and we are armed with data from the Birkman Method® assessment, there is nothing that can stop us from achieving our goals!

REFRAME
WHAT YOU NOW KNOW

- How emotionally intelligent are you?
- Do you consider yourself self-aware? How about in crowds?
- Can you get a feeling for the vibe or mood?
- Have you worked on your mindset at all?
- Do you know what your triggers and stress responses are?

As we learn about ourselves, we make it easier to live in our own skin. We can relate to others better, and we are confident communicators. And we can pursue our dreams and goals by having a solid understanding of ourselves and the world around us.

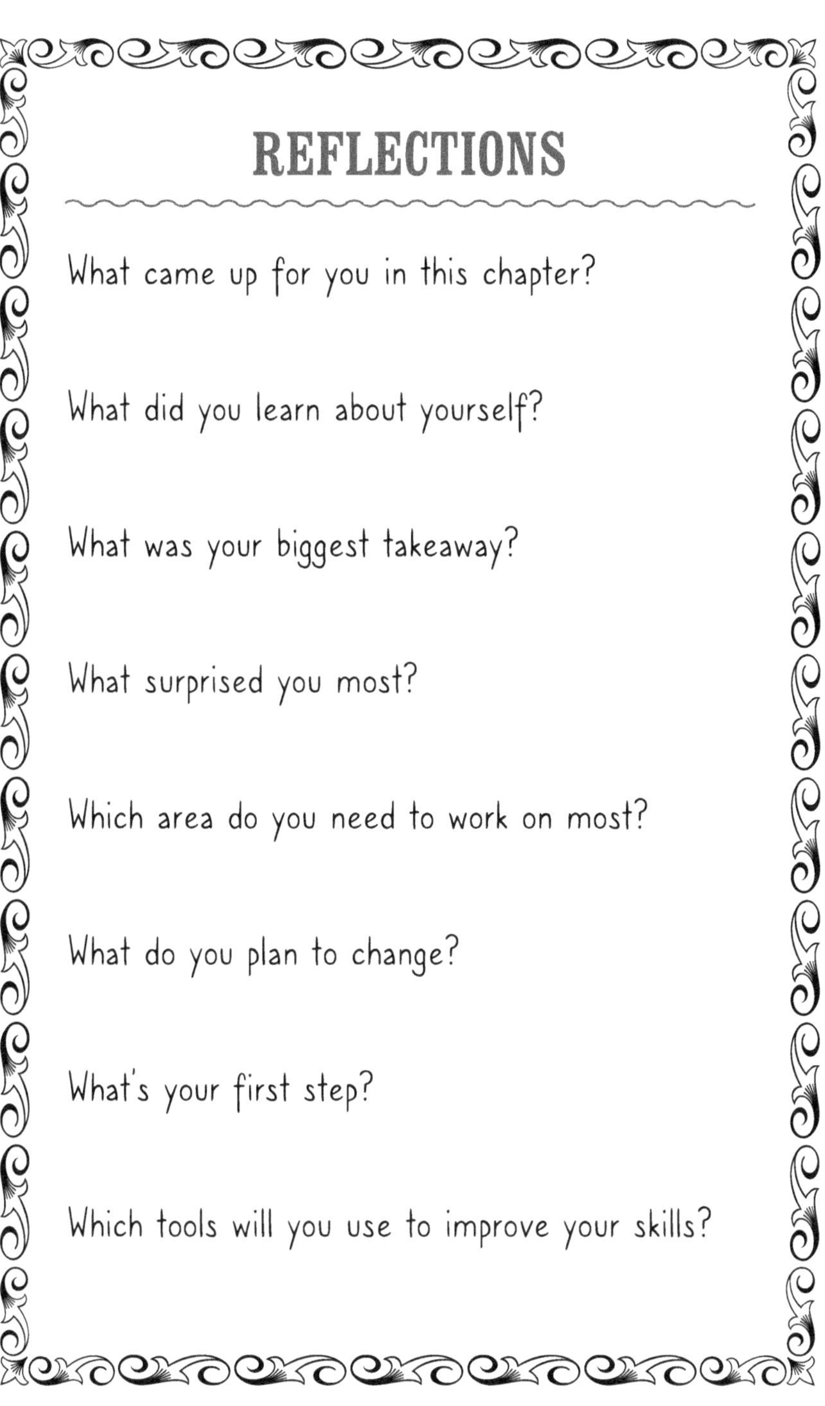

REFLECTIONS

What came up for you in this chapter?

What did you learn about yourself?

What was your biggest takeaway?

What surprised you most?

Which area do you need to work on most?

What do you plan to change?

What's your first step?

Which tools will you use to improve your skills?

CHAPTER THREE

STRESS AND LIMITING BELIEFS

"There is one grand lie: that we are limited. The only limits we have are the limits we believe."

– Wayne Dyer

Scenario:

Becky experiences a significant amount of distress whenever she is confronted or asked about anything at work. She has these old tapes of self-limiting beliefs playing in her head. So, she often finds herself saying (to herself), "I'm such a loser." "Why are they asking me? I don't know the answer. I never know!" "I wish I never got this job. I don't know what I'm doing." "I wish they would leave me alone." In other words, Becky is uncomfortable and scared most of the time when it comes to communicating with her colleagues.

To provide you with some context, Becky grew up in a family where her dad was the breadwinner, and her mom was the housemaker (stay-at-home mom). Her dad was a supervisor at a large car plant. He came home stressed a lot and would often yell at her mom and her.

Becky's brother died at age six, and her parents never got over it. They were depressed, and they both drank a lot of alcohol to cope with the pain.

As a result of the yelling, Becky became extremely introverted. She didn't want to get in her father's way, or he would yell at her and belittle her. Her dad often said things like, "women should be barefoot and pregnant," and "children should be seen and not heard."

At times it felt like verbal missiles were being shot across the room, so Becky did her best to duck and sneak quietly out of the room, not unlike her work behaviour.

Becky grew up believing women were undeserving of power, and she felt she was especially unworthy. So, she did not have big dreams or aspirations for herself. Becky carried this into her job because she did not put her name in for consideration whenever promotion opportunities came up. Despite that, her previous supervisor recommended her for a middle management position, which she hesitantly accepted. When she got promoted, she didn't dare tell her parents, or they would make her feel bad.

Becky doesn't believe women should be bosses or entrepreneurs, as women and power don't equate in her brain. Although she works in middle management, she feels undeserving of her promotion. She has a difficult time setting goals.

Becky believes she is a good person, but she doesn't believe she is worthy of having good things in life. She is subservient and has never spoken back to her parents or anyone with authority.

Much of Becky's limiting beliefs came from her parents. And after the trauma of her brother's death, she shut down emotionally. She didn't feel deserving of asking her parents for anything. Because before his death, her brother was the "golden child," and she was just "Becky."

Being shy, Becky does not take great care in her appearance, as she does not want to bring attention to herself. So she combs her hair, puts it in a ponytail, and leaves for work. Becky doesn't wear any makeup or perfume, and she avoids having her photograph taken. She has horrible eye contact, and for the most part, she stands and sits in a slouched position.

Becky lacks passion, so she doesn't really like her job. She does it because she doesn't think she can get better. Plus, Becky doesn't know what type of job would bring her joy. And even if she did know what brought her joy, would she be deserving of it?

For the most part, Becky feels somewhat content with her life and has zero desire to change anything. She knows she is not happy, but changing terrifies her.

This chapter will look at how living with stress and suffering with limiting beliefs impacts our bodies and our minds. We will begin with a quiz that will help you determine your limiting beliefs, as they may negatively impact your ability to communicate and manage conflict effectively.

SELF-LIMITING BELIEFS – QUIZ

As you can see, Becky has self-limiting beliefs that hold her back in life. She lacks confidence and feels she is unworthy. Her limiting beliefs also negatively impact her ability to communicate effectively, both verbally and through her body language.

Do you see yourself in Becky?

Take a moment to answer these questions to see if you can

identify **your self-limiting beliefs** and **how they impact your communication style**. It's best to be as honest as possible.

- **What do you believe about yourself?**
  - Are you a good person or a bad person?
  - Do you feel worthy of having good things in life?
  - What are your strengths?
  - Introvert? Extrovert?
  - What are your beliefs about women in top career positions?
  - Are you depressed?
  - Do you feel like you are not as good as others?

- **Why do you believe this about yourself?**
  - Where did you get this belief?
  - Is your belief from a parent or other person of authority (teacher)?
  - Did you have trauma at any point in your life?

- **How has this impacted your life?**
  - If you feel poorly about yourself, what has this done to you?
  - How does it impact conflicts with others?
  - Are you doing the job you love, or are you just getting by?
  - Are you as successful in your life as you want to be (using your definition of success)?

- **Are you willing to change?**
  - What does this mean for you?

  - Where could you be one year from now? Five years from now?
  - Are you willing to do the work?
  - What do you need to change?
  - Get professional help? Hire a coach?

- **What can you do?**
  - Calm your brain during stress or conflict
  - How do you feel about your answers? Does anything surprise you?

SELF-LIMITING BELIEFS – WHAT IS IT?

WHAT ARE SELF-LIMITING BELIEFS?

Success Magazine says, “When it comes to building an incredible life, there is no limit to what you can do. The only thing keeping you from reaching your potential is a lack of self-belief.”[6]

As you can see with Becky’s example, self-limiting beliefs impacted her ability to communicate effectively. She doesn’t know what lights her up and doesn’t feel worthy of living her dream life anyway. She is afraid to ask for what she wants. For the most part, she wants to remain invisible, as it’s safer. She is unaware her limiting beliefs are holding her back from being truly happy.

Therefore, it’s essential to learn what self-limiting beliefs are and how they can be changed.

Our beliefs are formed starting at a young age. We are continuously subjected to information from the dominant people

---

[6] https://medium.com/@successmagazine/15-quotes-to-overcome-your-self-limiting-beliefs-15f2658d751c

in our lives, causing us to process the information to stay safe. This is done by recognizing patterns and creating associations between things. Based on our experiences, we form certain beliefs. For example, if we do something considered "wrong" or "bad," we are punished.

Our beliefs become more complex as we get older, as we can draw on more information and data from movies, television shows, books, and media we are exposed to. Additionally, how our peer group behaves also impacts our beliefs.

Our original "old" beliefs become our core beliefs and stay with us for life even when new data is introduced. As such, our core beliefs become very powerful and difficult to change, even when they hold us back in life.

Why? For one, we have gone our entire life believing something. If we need to accept new data as fact, it means we were wrong this entire time. Most of us don't like being "wrong" about anything! So the ego is at play here. However, the other reason is we have gone our entire life searching for evidence that supports our core beliefs and which ultimately makes us "right."

The more toxic the environment we were exposed to growing up, the more likely we are to have self-limiting beliefs. But even those who grew up in loving environments may have some limiting beliefs. Limiting beliefs can cause us a tremendous amount of stress.

Beliefs are limiting when they hold us back from pursuing our dreams and goals. Beliefs don't have to be based on fact, and they certainly don't have to be true. They have to be something we believe to be real. The critical thing to recognize is our beliefs affect our thoughts, which affect our behaviour and choices. So, if we want to make better decisions and improve our behaviour, we need to unpack our beliefs and tell ourselves a different story.

HOW TO CHANGE OUR BELIEFS

A belief may have served us in life to keep us safe but, if it's causing us harm or holding us back from being happy, it's time to address it. We need to think about why the belief exists, when it started, and ask if it is still true for us. What was true when we were 10 or 15 is no longer true for us now. We need to look at our successes—not our failures. If we look at what we've done instead of what we have not done, we will be better able to change our stories and beliefs.

There is no reason to feel shame or blame during this process, as our beliefs were there to serve a purpose. We can laugh at how silly it may seem now and decide it's something we no longer want to carry. We can even thank it and say goodbye. Then we can create a new belief to replace it.

For example, instead of saying, "If I'm not perfect, nobody will like me," we can replace it with "I'm doing my best, and that is enough." We can create affirmations from the new beliefs and repeat them often to help train our brains to create new neural pathways.

Can you imagine how limiting beliefs can impact your communication? If you believed you were not worthy of great things, you would be less likely to be able to ask for what you want. Volunteering on projects or teams would be difficult. And when called on to speak about your ideas, you may feel uncomfortable and hold back. Your beliefs could act as a mute, holding you back from fully articulating what you think or your recommendations.

With limiting beliefs, you may be shy to fight for what you want. You could have brilliant ideas locked up inside your brain, but you are too afraid to share them with anyone, in fear of what they will think or say.

Or, like Becky, it could impact your confidence and sense of self-worth.

We've looked at how limiting beliefs affect our ability to communicate. Now let's look at the impact stress has on lives and our ability to communicate effectively.

LIVING WITH STRESS

First of all, we need to recognize the significance and seriousness of stress, as the World Health Organization classifies it as the "health epidemic of the 21st century."[7]

As stress can create a disturbance in our mental and physical well-being, it can impact our ability to communicate effectively.

We all know life can be complicated, and it can be stressful—even during the best of times! For example, workplace situations can cause stress, including getting inadequate feedback, having unrealistic expectations, making assumptions, and lacking priorities or goals. And then there is the dreaded "bad boss" who can make our work life genuinely miserable!

MAJOR LIFE EVENTS AND STRESSORS

Unfortunately, most of us will experience one or more of the following major life stressors:

- Death of a partner
- Loss of a child
- Marriage/divorce
- Birth of a child/grandchild
- Loss of a job/new job
- Health problems
- Abuse
- Financial problems
- Legal problems
- Retirement

---

7 https://hcatodayblog.com/2019/04/30/stress-the-health-epidemic-of-the-21st-century/

SIGNS OF EMOTIONAL STRESS

Some of us are so used to experiencing stress, it becomes "normal" for us. But we need to be aware of how stress impacts us in our body with the following emotional signs of stress:

- Becoming overly emotional or aggressive
- Feeling overwhelmed or immense pressure
- Experiencing frustration over little things
- Loss of interest in personal appearance or previously enjoyed activities
- Poor concentration or focus
- Irrational mood swings (feeling up and then down)
- Feeling anxious
- Inability to make decisions
- Experiencing sadness, guilt, or fatigue
- Loss of confidence in personal ability to do the work
- Low self-esteem or lack of confidence

Do any of those stress responses sound familiar? If so, consider how it impacts your ability to even think about what you want to say, let alone say it! Stress takes over our thought processes, making it difficult for us to show up at work as our "best selves."

HOW OUR BODY RESPONDS TO STRESS

Now consider what happens in our body when we are stressed:

- Dilation of pupils
- Sweating
- Rapid breathing
- Increase in heart rate

- Muscle tension
- Increased adrenaline flow
- Release of glucose into the blood
- Decrease in gut activity
- Decrease in salivation

If you are experiencing any of the above-listed signs or symptoms, speak to a healthcare professional, as holding on to stress in your body can be very unhealthy for you. Long-term stress factors include high blood pressure, heart disease, depression, anxiety, panic attacks, and erratic behaviour.

Can you imagine trying to have effective communication at work while experiencing any of these signs or symptoms of stress? What if you need to have a difficult conversation? Do you think your ability to deal with conflict effectively will be compromised?

If you answered *yes*, then you get it!

Now let's look at what you can do to mitigate the stress.

Researchers have found being around negative people can kill you. So this is no laughing matter. "A UCLA study of 122 healthy adults found that those with negative social experiences had higher levels of pro-inflammatory proteins, which could lead to depression, hypertension, atherosclerosis, coronary heart disease, diabetes, and cancer."[8]

Having long anger episodes can increase our blood pressure, bring on stress and anxiety, trigger headaches, and cause poor circulation. It can also weaken our immune system, which puts us at risk for serious illnesses such as depression, stroke, and a heart attack.

Cardiologist and contributor to the *Huff Post* wrote, "Research also shows even one five-minute episode of anger is so stressful it

---

[8] https://www.insider.com/signs-of-a-bad-friendship-health-2018-5

can impair your immune system for more than six hours. All of these health issues can lead to more serious problems such as heart attacks and stroke. Anger and hatred can be directed at yourself or at other people, but either way you lose when you allow these negative foods for the soul to take over.[9]

With this in mind, it's essential to evaluate your relationships. Are they serving you well? Or are they dragging you down?

OUR BRAIN'S STRESS RESPONSE

Anything you think of that scares you can be a threat or fear in your mind. Your stress response helps you to jump out of the way of a moving car or run out of a burning home. But when your stress response happens chronically over time, it can wreak havoc on your body's systems.

However, the inner conflict especially wreaks havoc on our brains and, more specifically, the amygdala. The amygdala, located at the front of the brain, detects fear. It then releases adrenaline and cortisol throughout the body, preparing us for "fight, flight, or freeze."

Because the brain's prefrontal cortex is essentially hijacked, it shuts down the neural pathway, causing our nervous system to kick in, provoking our old protective mechanism to take over, making rational decision-making impossible. Whew! That sounds like a lot of activity inside our minds and bodies that we are not even aware of!

That's why, if you experienced trauma as a child and your response was to hide in the corner, as an adult, your body will respond similarly whenever your brain perceives a threat.

If we know our brains and bodies respond to conflict using a conditioned response, the key to gaining control of our lives is to

---

[9] https://www.huffpost.com/entry/emotional-wellness_b_4612392

be mindful and present. Also, being aware of tools and techniques we can use in stressful times will help to prevent us from going into fear, flight, or freeze response, as we have done earlier in life.

HOW WOULD YOU REACT DURING A STRESSFUL SITUATION AT WORK?

What would your stress response be, given this type of situation?

> *Your colleague approaches you and starts freaking out because she was asked to take on a project she "doesn't care about" and "quite frankly doesn't have time for!" This is the first time you hear about the project, but it seems like a great learning opportunity, so you don't understand your colleague's reaction.*
>
> *As she is yelling, you can feel your heart beating faster and louder. You know your colleague would not hurt you. But your legs are starting to cramp up, and you feel like you want to get up and leave the room. Your head is spinning, so you are finding it difficult to follow what she is saying. Your palms are getting sweaty.*
>
> *You were in the middle of working on an important project when she rudely interrupted you, but you wouldn't dare tell her to stop. You are aware you feel like you did when your grade one teacher used to yell at you, pull on your ear, and berate you in class in front of the other students.*
>
> *So you focus on taking some deep breaths, taking in the smell of essential oils on your desk as you feel your lungs fill up with air. You think of a tree as you plant your feet into the floor, and you adjust your buttocks as you sit at your desk. You tell yourself that you are a grown woman at work (you are not the scared little kid whose ear was pulled at by your mean grade one teacher). As you are engaging some of your senses, you*

work your way through your grounding techniques. You start to feel your body and mind begin to calm down. Crisis averted!

Would you have responded like the person in this example? Or would you have flipped out on your colleague?

WHAT YOU CAN DO ABOUT WORKPLACE STRESS

If you are experiencing stress in the workplace, take a few minutes to relax. You can do deep breathing, roll your shoulders, and do some light stretches. You could also do a brief meditation at your desk or escape to a quiet place for five to ten minutes.

Another option to explore is addressing the root cause of your stress by speaking with your manager, counsellor or coach. Perhaps you need support or clarification on a project.

You can control the flow of work by chunking out your schedule and using time management techniques. Plus, eliminating or reducing distractions is also helpful.

Look at your work-life balance. If you work overtime a lot, stop it. Don't forget to have laughter and joy in your life. Connect with friends, listen to music, dance, and have fun.

"You begin to fly when you let go of self-limiting beliefs and allow your mind and aspirations to rise to greater heights."

– Brian Tracy

IN CONCLUSION

As you can see, what we think and believe about ourselves, and how much stress we are coping with, greatly impacts our ability to communicate and manage conflict effectively. In our next chapter, we will visit communication styles and what our typical responses are so we can learn to course correct.

REFRAME
WHAT YOU NOW KNOW

Hopefully, after reading this chapter, you recognize how stress can significantly impact our bodies and minds. What's more, stress influences how we think and feel, causing us to react in ways that are not productive and could actually be harmful to our relationships. So, if we don't learn how to manage stress, it will be easy for us to overreact and say the wrong thing.

If you haven't done so already, I strongly encourage you to complete the self-limiting beliefs quiz. As you could see from the scenario with Becky, her personality was impacted by her limiting beliefs.

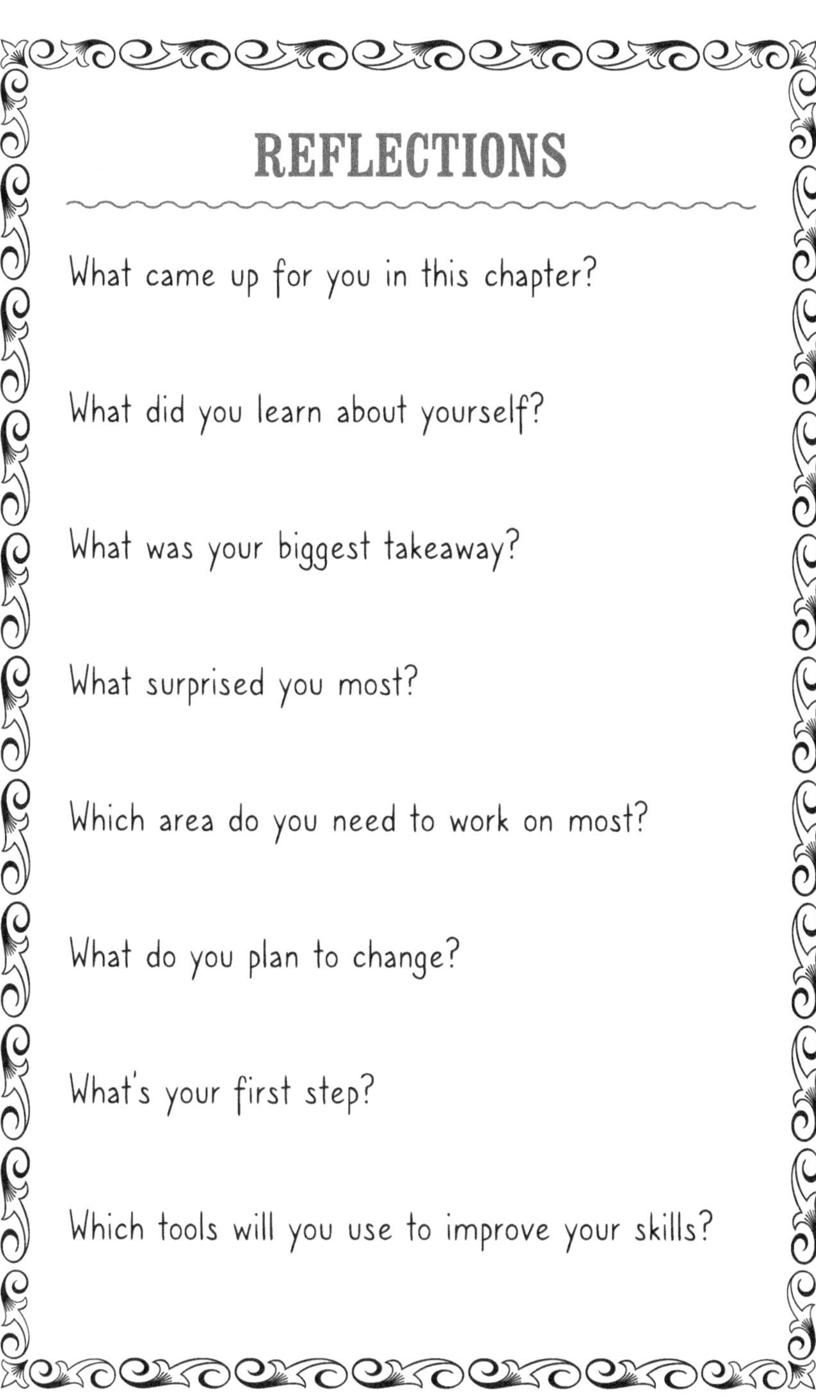

REFLECTIONS

What came up for you in this chapter?

What did you learn about yourself?

What was your biggest takeaway?

What surprised you most?

Which area do you need to work on most?

What do you plan to change?

What's your first step?

Which tools will you use to improve your skills?

CHAPTER FOUR

COMMUNICATION STYLES AND OUR RESPONSES

"To effectively communicate, we must realize that we are all different in the way we perceive the world and use this understanding as a guide to our communication with others."

– Tony Robbins

This chapter will review what your typical reactions may be to a conflict or unpleasant situation. We will also look at communication styles and cycles that interfere with our ability to resolve conflict amicably and productively.

When I am in front of my class, my first question is always, "Who here loves conflict?" The response is the same each time. No one raises their hand. That is, no one except me.

Many people react poorly because of their fear of conflict. Often, we are unprepared for an attack. And because there was no preparation, it feels like conflict comes from out of the blue.

Do you tend to avoid conflict like the plague? Or do you dig right in with your first reaction?

While reading through the following responses to conflict, check in with yourself to see if you identify with any of these scenarios, and imagine how you could reframe your responses going forward.

I have provided you with examples demonstrating the "wrong" reaction versus the "right" response. Use these different scenarios to identify where you may correct how you respond in similar situations.

Much of what I will share in this chapter, I learned from the textbook, *Managing Conflict Through Communication* by Dudley D. Cahn and Ruth Anna Abigail. I used this book when I taught the Conflict Management course at Trinity Western University.

The students and I enjoyed the content, as it related to real issues that happen in life. Our discussions were often quite lively, as the students were fascinated by learning about how our behaviour and personalities impact our ability to communicate and manage conflict.

REFRAMING OUR RESPONSES TO CONFLICT

Blame Others/Blame Yourself

Blaming responses are not helpful. They will lead to a disintegration of the relationship over time.

Details	What Blaming Looks Like	A Positive Reframe
One of the first reactions to conflict is to blame others.	"That wasn't me. I didn't do that. Janet, in accounting, did not give me the papers I needed on time."	"You're right. I own this. I did not get the papers and follow up on this."
Another reaction would be you would blame the person who is attacking you.	"Well, if you would have done what you were supposed to do, I would have done what I was supposed to do."	"It looks like we both may have slipped up on this one. So how can we start again?"
The flipside of this is for someone who accepts blame themselves because of their low self-esteem and lack of confidence.	"I know; I am sorry. It won't happen again."	"You know what? I'm going to look into this. This doesn't seem right. I will look into it, and I will get back to you by one o'clock."

Figure 2. Douma, Y. (2021). *Reframe: How to Change Your Conversations to Resolve Those Messy Conflicts.*

Defend Yourself

Defending yourself is another common reaction.

Details	What Defending Looks Like	A Positive Reframe
Not taking responsibility for the situation	"I was so busy today."	"I let today get away from me. Would it be okay if I were to get this report to you by tomorrow morning?"
Not taking responsibility for the situation	"I got stuck in traffic."	"I didn't leave early enough to consider heavy traffic."

Figure 3. Douma, Y. (2021). *Reframe: How to Change Your Conversations to Resolve Those Messy Conflicts.*

Get into an Angry Rage

Angry people do not like to be confronted with any critical feedback. They would attack the other person, even if they were trying to give the feedback in a gentle manner.

Details	What an Angry Rage Looks Like	A Positive Reframe
You could expect a response with a loud, angry voice.	"Are you freaking kidding me?"	Take a deep breath and say, "Can you tell me more?" or "Can you give me an example?"
There are also a lot of "you" statements.	"You always leave the dishes in the sink!"	"I noticed that dishes are being left in the sink a lot. So, I'm just reminding everyone to stay on top of it so we don't get fruit flies."
There are accusations and deflection.	"You do it too!"	"Yes, I could do better. At this time, we are not talking about me."

Figure 4. Douma, Y. (2021). *Reframe: How to Change Your Conversations to Resolve Those Messy Conflicts*.

Give the Silent Treatment

And then some people just shut down. They feel they have been unjustly accused and refuse to talk to the other person. They may even leave the house without saying anything, leaving the other person worried about where they are.

Details	What the Silent Treatment Looks Like	A Positive Reframe
They don't speak anymore, sometimes for days. They give dirty looks.	Radio silence	"Now is not a safe time. Just give me some time, and we can talk about it when I have processed this."

Figure 5. Douma, Y. (2021). *Reframe: How to Change Your Conversations to Resolve Those Messy Conflicts*.

Threaten

And then some people make threats.

Details	What Threatening Looks Like	A Positive Reframe
Someone is feeling threatened, so they attack first. They could be throwing things around or hitting objects.	"Oh, you think this is bad. Just wait until I really show you what mad is."	"We need to talk about this; however, now would not be a good time. Let's both give each other some time to cool down, okay?"

Figure 6. Douma, Y. (2021). *Reframe: How to Change Your Conversations to Resolve Those Messy Conflicts*.

COMMUNICATION STYLES AND CYCLES

In the last section, I shared specific examples of bad versus good responses (e.g., blaming, defending) so you can see how to reframe a conversation. In this next section, we'll look at our communication patterns, more specifically our communication styles and communication cycles, to identify and correct specific issues we have.

DYSFUNCTIONAL CONFLICT CYCLES

Dysfunctional conflict cycles are scripted events that have an undesired repetitive pattern. These cycles can cause us to feel trapped in circumstances beyond our control. As we are unconscious to dysfunctional conflict cycles, we often experience knee-jerk responses. And because they occur without intention, they can often cause a situation to escalate out of control.[10]

We get insight into the blind spots and knee-jerk reactions many of us are unaware of with dysfunctional conflict cycles.

---

[10] Cahn, D. D. & Abigail, R.A. *Managing Conflict Through Communication, 5th Edition.* New York. Pearson Publisher. 2014

We also gain insights into our own dysfunctional conflict styles. Knowing this helps us to mitigate future conflicts. For example, by understanding our triggers, we can role play in our minds to respond better the next time we have a conflict.

This section will be looking at the three most common dysfunctional communication styles: avoiding/accommodating, competitive, and passive-aggressive.

As you read the following examples, ask yourself if you exhibit any of these behaviours. Or does someone you know (boss, colleague, partner) exhibit these behaviours?

AVOIDING/ACCOMMODATING CONFLICT – COMMUNICATION STYLE AND CYCLE

One style of communicating through conflict is by avoiding or accommodating. We often do this to avoid embarrassment. One of our greatest fears is to appear stupid to other people. Another reason to avoid conflict is we don't want to offend anyone. However, when we accommodate, we hold onto resentful feelings. Using this communication style leads to hidden anger, which will eventually blow up.

- By *avoiding* the situation, we do our best not to engage with the conflict. But if they insist, we are likely to give in quickly.
- By *accommodating* the situation, we try to smooth things over, obliging others not to make any waves.

Examples of the Avoiding/Accommodating Conflict Communication *Style*:[11]

- "I don't dare say anything."

---

[11] Cahn, D. D. & Abigail, R.A. *Managing Conflict Through Communication, 5th Edition.* New York. Pearson Publisher. 2014

- "I do not want this to get awkward."
- "What good would it do? No one listens anyway."
- "I don't want to offend anyone."
- "Whatever you decide is okay with me."

Avoiding/Accommodating Conflict Communication *Cycle* looks like this:[12]

- People think confrontation is bad, and avoiding it is the best thing.
- Confrontation makes us nervous.
- If something makes us nervous, we need to put it off.
- If not dealt with, issues become worse.
- Anxiety causes us to deal with it poorly.
- Because the conflict turns out poorly, it confirms conflict is bad.
- It can escalate to gunnysacking.

Scenario:

Maria and Samantha both work as legal assistants in a busy downtown firm. Marie is relatively new, soft-spoken, and trying desperately to fit into the corporate culture. Samantha, on the other hand, is a social butterfly. She spends more time gossiping and visiting her friends. Samantha has been getting behind on her work because of her social escapades. The past few weeks, she's asked Maria to cover for her and do her work as well. Maria is new, and she's not comfortable with conflict, so she just nods. Even though Maria has been noticing an

[12] Cahn, D. D. & Abigail, R.A. *Managing Conflict Through Communication, 5th Edition.* New York. Pearson Publisher. 2014

increase in her stress, she's terribly uncomfortable speaking up, in fear Samantha won't like her (or will complain Maria is not a team player). So Maria suffers in silence.

GUNNYSACKING

What is gunnysacking? When we use avoidance/accommodating communication style, repressed frustrations can build over time. We end up storing grievances. So the "nice person," who never complains and does everything they are asked, despite how they may feel inside, eventually explodes. It's essentially the straw that broke the camel's back. It's not a pretty sight!

Gunnysacking is highly emotional. And holding onto this stress and anger wreaks havoc on our system. When we are stressed, our nervous system releases stress hormones such as cortisone and adrenaline into our bodies. When we hold onto this type of toxic emotion, we can increase our blood pressure and heart rate, putting us at risk for a blood clot.[13]

Even though we may have a ton of hurts to bring up, remember it's best to deal with only one conflict at a time.

What does gunnysacking look like?[14]

- We store up hurts and anger until we explode.
- When we are in conflict, we do not stick to the one conflict/situation. Instead, we add other past conflicts to build up our case.
- We talk from a perspective the other person doesn't understand.

---

[13] https://www.health.harvard.edu/heart-health/from-irritated-to-enraged-angers-toxic-effect-on-the-heart

[14] Cahn, D. D. & Abigail, R.A. *Managing Conflict Through Communication, 5th Edition.* New York. Pearson Publisher. 2014

- Often the other person does not even know they are bothering us.

Scenario:

Jason and Richard have been working late for the last several weeks. They are tired, have brain fog, and are both feeling guilty they aren't with their families more. Towards the end of one evening, they both had had it. Jason told Richard he was sick of Richard leaving him to do all the shutdown of operations EVERY night. Richard responded, "Really? You leave me with all the photocopying and scanning every night." Jason replied, "Wow! I can't believe this."

Here we have two men who are overworked and exhausted. Most of the time, they get along great, but the stress of them overworking and not seeing their families is too great. Jason and Richard continued to argue and fight, and yell about past scenarios. "Well, you did this. And this. And this." Not helpful. What could they have done differently? They could have recognized they were both tired, and had a chat. They could have discussed how they were feeling and shared the stress the overtime was having on them. They could have discussed how they could help each other to limit the stress. Perhaps they could have agreed to look at what was happening and devise a different plan. They could have had each other's back instead of having the additional stress of them fighting, on top of everything they were going through.

COMPETITIVE – CONFLICT COMMUNICATION STYLE AND CYCLE

We have all been there. Conflict can often lead to tense conversations. One person starts to speak louder, the other person speaks even louder, and so on. This happens with two strong-willed people who do not want to give up ground. These often lead to unresolvable conflicts, and relationships tend to take a beating, especially since there is so much hurt.

With this type of communication style, we are so concerned with winning (or being "right"), we have no desire to listen to the other person's point of view.

This is a lose/lose style of communication. No one wins. There is just hurt. It gets hidden for a while until it blows up again.

When our desire to express our opinion turns into our need to win the argument, it becomes competitive. We don't allow any space for the other person to express their thoughts or feelings to us. We don't give them equal consideration.

COMPETITIVE CONFLICT COMMUNICATION STYLE:[15]

- Talking louder
- Yelling
- Standing up
- Getting into each other's space
- Making a threatening gesture

COMPETITIVE CONFLICT COMMUNICATION CYCLE:[16]

- There are previous unresolved hurts or grievances.
- I'm right; you are wrong.
- It intensifies when the other responds; also with a win/lose idea.
- The outcome is to win/lose.

---

[15] Cahn, D. D. & Abigail, R.A. *Managing Conflict Through Communication, 5th Edition*. New York. Pearson Publisher. 2014

[16] Cahn, D. D. & Abigail, R.A. *Managing Conflict Through Communication, 5th Edition*. New York. Pearson Publisher. 2014

- The loser still holds unresolved grievances that affect future conflicts.
- Another scenario is outlined below.

Scenario:

Derek and Justin have a history of being competitive when pitching project proposals from opposite teams. But their boss recently assigned them to the same pitch team. Many of the staff have complained to each other about Justin's aggressive attitude, as he tends to bully his colleagues into getting his way. Derek came up with a winning idea he knew his boss would approve. He pitched it during their staff meeting, and Justin tried to take credit. Derek said, "Dude, you know this was my idea." Justin said with a loud voice, "What the heck, Derek; you trying to call me a liar?" Derek, now shouting, responds, "If the shoe fits!" The boss is not happy about how quickly it escalated, so he takes them to his office for a chat. NOT ACCEPTABLE BEHAVIOUR!

PASSIVE-AGGRESSIVE COMMUNICATION STYLE:

The passive-aggressive communication style is downright mean, as it is done with malicious intent. When we employ this communication style, we impose our will onto others by verbal or nonverbal acts. Although our behaviour may appear to avoid an open conflict and accommodate the other person's needs, we use this style to inflict pain (physical or psychological), injury, or suffering on the other person.[17]

---

[17] Cahn, D. D. & Abigail, R.A. *Managing Conflict Through Communication, 5th Edition.* New York. Pearson Publisher. 2014

PASSIVE-AGGRESSIVE COMMUNICATION STYLE:[18]

- Someone says something you disagree with.
- Your heart starts beating. Your physiological responses start happening.
- You get your back up (become defensive).
- One person starts to speak and says something.
- The other person speaks louder, and so on.
- Both people think they are right and are not willing to give up ground.

PASSIVE-AGGRESSIVE COMMUNICATION CYCLE:[19]

- Conflict is bad, and we should avoid it.
- It makes us nervous.
- Put off as long as possible.
- He goes behind the person's back to get his way.
- If we get our way, our behaviour is confirmed, and the cycle starts again.

As the passive-aggressive communication style is incredibly destructive, it will be covered in more detail in Chapter six.

ASSUMPTIONS/PERCEPTIONS AS A THOUGHT PROCESS

Many of us believe our situation is not normal and our circumstances are worse than everyone else's. But we don't know what other people are experiencing in their lives. They may present with

[18] Cahn, D. D. & Abigail, R.A. *Managing Conflict Through Communication, 5th Edition.* New York. Pearson Publisher. 2014

[19] Cahn, D. D. & Abigail, R.A. *Managing Conflict Through Communication, 5th Edition.* New York. Pearson Publisher. 2014

a happy demeanour, but they could actually be suffering inside. Also, we can't control anyone's actions. We can only control our reactions to them.

Unfortunately, conflict is going to happen everywhere. And our reactions are what is going to make or break this conflict. Moreover, our responses are going to make or break our relationships!

This thought process can escalate as follows:

- Something negative happens.
- We didn't confront or ask the person.
- We make an assumption.
- We get angry (the other person may not even be aware).
- We know everything—we are right and justified for our feelings.
- We become passive-aggressive.

As you can see, these types of assumptions and perceptions become a precursor for passive-aggressive behaviour.

WORKPLACE SCENARIO

To look at what the cycle would be for the assumptions/perceptions communication style, let's use an example of one of our colleagues who had a tough morning before arriving at work:

Michelle had a sleepless night. As a result, she slept in late for work. Her kids were uncooperative, and the youngest was downright naughty. Just as she was leaving the house, her husband picked a fight with her about something that could have been discussed later. To pour salt in the wounds, she got pulled over for speeding while driving to work so she could not make it in time for her meeting.

Clearly, Michelle had a difficult morning, which is why we need to remember it's not always about us! When Michelle comes into work and her body language is negative, or she forgets to say "good morning," it's best not to assume she is mad at you. The truth is, it's more likely she's not thinking about you at all. We can give some space and grace to Michelle. How we respond determines what our relationship will be in the future. So be kind, and don't assume.

We could say, "Michelle, I noticed you slammed your door when you came in today. I was just checking on you to make sure you're okay. Is there anything you need?" This type of check-in allows people the space and grace to calm down, while calling them out on their behaviour. Not addressing it enables the negative behaviour to continue.

CONFLICT RATING SCALE

Take a look at the chart to see how you usually deal with conflict.

Now think about your last conflict. How did you deal with it? Rate yourself.

Rating	Conflict Response Description
1	Identify the problem and accept your role in it
2	Solve the problem together, looking at both sides of the issue
3	Rarely complain about anything and want to help others
4	Complain a bit, back down easily, and harbour some resentment
5	Start to show resentment by not doing certain things for other people
6	Show resentment often and do and say things to hurt other people
7	Say mean things out loud or yell
8	Say mean things whenever you can, yelling and never backing down
9	Almost physically attack but hold back at last moment
10	Physical attack

Figure 7. Douma, Y. (2021). *Reframe: How to Change Your Conversations to Resolve Those Messy Conflicts.*

DESCRIPTION:

- 1–2 collaborative
- 3–4 passive
- 5–6 passive-aggressive
- 7–8–9 loud and demeaning words
- 10 physically aggressive

> ***MINI-DISCLAIMER:***
>
> ***As I am not a medical doctor, this chart is NOT to be used to diagnose yourself with a condition. It is to be used for informational purposes only.***

"Words are singularly the most powerful force available to humanity. We can choose to use this force constructively with words of encouragement, or destructively using words of despair. Words have energy and power with the ability to help, to heal, to hinder, to hurt, to harm, to humiliate and to humble."

– Yehuda Berg

IN CONCLUSION

This chapter reviewed various communication styles and cycles that can be problematic. When we use effective communication in our everyday life, we respect ourselves and those we are communicating with. And when we understand the mechanics of conflict, we will be able to avoid it like a pro!

In the next chapter, we will learn how to have difficult conversations.

REFRAME WHAT YOU NOW KNOW

Our communication style is based on learned behaviour. Knowing this, we can choose other ways to communicate in a way that nurtures our relationships instead of harming them. The choice is ours.

Hopefully, you were able to identify the responses to a conflict that resonates with you, to learn to reframe them into a more effective communication technique.

And if you recognize yourself in any of the communication styles, you could identify what happens during the cycle so you can make better choices to avoid escalation.

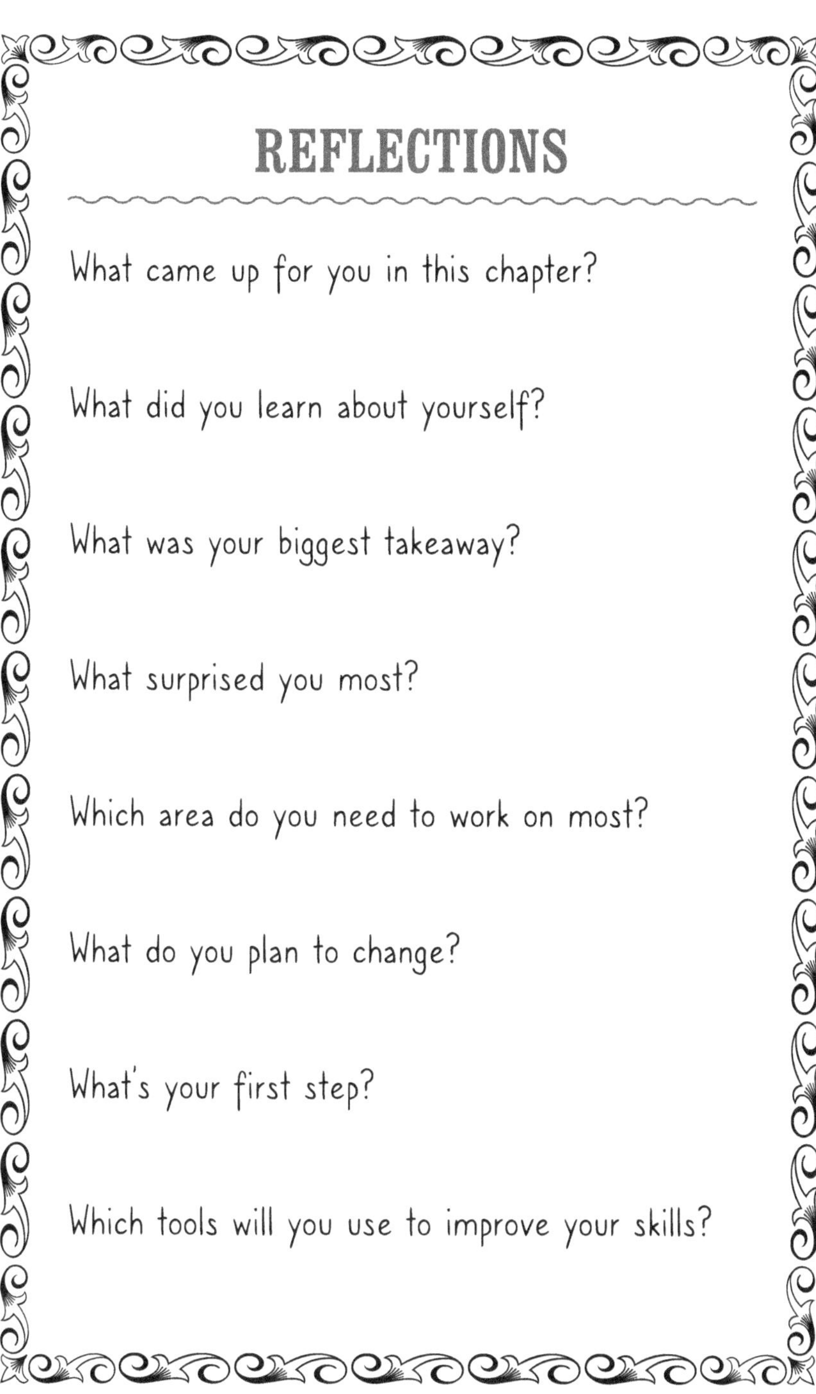

REFLECTIONS

What came up for you in this chapter?

What did you learn about yourself?

What was your biggest takeaway?

What surprised you most?

Which area do you need to work on most?

What do you plan to change?

What's your first step?

Which tools will you use to improve your skills?

CHAPTER FIVE

DIFFICULT CONVERSATIONS

"When we avoid difficult conversations, we trade short-term discomfort for long-term dysfunction."

- Peter Bromberg

In this chapter, we will look at the art of mastering difficult conversations. Why? Because acquiring this skillset can truly transform your life! Don't let the word "difficult" scare you, as I have provided you with an understanding of what difficult conversations are. More importantly, I have broken down for you how to prepare and implement difficult conversations. Seriously, the techniques you learn in this chapter WILL have a positive impact on your relationships. That is, if you do the work.

Throughout my career, I have referred to the ultimate resource, *Difficult Conversations*[20], to help others learn how to do conflict

---

[20] Stone, D., Patton, B., & Heen, S. Difficult Conversations: How to Discuss What Matters Most. London, Penguin Books Limited, 1999.

well. This book teaches people how to go from negatively reacting in situations, to stopping and thinking through the process before spouting off at the mouth.

Teaching how to have difficult conversations was my favourite thing to do as a teacher and in my consulting practice. There were so many "aha" moments and practical advice learners could apply immediately. I'm confident after you read this book, you will think about some of the previous conflicts you have had, and you will realize how you could have done things differently. It's okay, as you can still "fix" any relationships you may have caused harm by having difficult conversations. As you read through this chapter, you will learn some basic ideas you can implement now.

This chapter was inspired by Stone et al. (1999), who have greatly influenced my career and helped me to not only teach others but also use the techniques to strengthen my relationships.

HOW ARE YOUR WORK RELATIONSHIPS?

Workplace Scenario:

You love your job and, for the most part, you like your colleagues. But whenever you start talking in a meeting, your marketing counterpart rudely interrupts and starts to talk over you. She has a habit of never letting you finish your point. She does this repeatedly. Up until now, you didn't want to say anything because you are new to the company.

However, you are starting to feel resentment towards her. You take pride in managing positive workplace relationships, and you are afraid you will blow up at her the next time she interrupts you. So, you realize you need to have a difficult conversation with her. Now what?

Uncomfortable and painful situations are quite common. The quality of our work relationships and how we feel about certain people at work indicate how much workplace stress we are carrying. How do you feel about your workplace? Is there any unwanted "drama?"

- What are you experiencing at work?
- Do you feel disrespected, dismissed, or unappreciated?
- Are you frustrated you were not put up for promotion?
- Do you avoid speaking up in meetings?
- Is work stress starting to affect your health or your relationships at home negatively?

If you have answered *yes* to any of these questions, then reading this book can and will help you.

This chapter will look at how critical it is to use effective communication to validate and understand. And you will learn how to have a difficult conversation so you improve your relationships at work (and home).

WHAT IS A DIFFICULT CONVERSATION?

In short, a difficult conversation is any conversation we are not looking forward to having.

For example, are you being bullied at work by a colleague? Is someone repeatedly getting in your face? Is your employee not measuring up? Has your boss been criticizing your work performance in public?

If so, you need to have a difficult conversation to remedy the situation and improve your workplace relationships.

People often avoid the situation, which makes them feel insecure, miserable, and stressed. Even some feel like they are an imposter, like they can't do the job.

If you are experiencing resistance to the thought of having a difficult conversation, then you likely need to have one, or two, or even three!

Now is the time to get honest with yourself. If you've ever been unhappy with a situation at work, and you knew the only way it would get better is if you confronted the situation head on—but still, you were too afraid—then learning how to have a difficult conversation will help you.

No worries. You are not alone. Our fear of conflict is often greater than our desire to resolve the situation, which is why many people continue to be unhappy in their current jobs without doing anything about it. So they continue to feel stuck in a position that causes them stress or pain. But it doesn't have to be that way!

What if we could learn how to communicate and have difficult conversations where both parties felt heard and respected? What if we felt comfortable speaking with our boss about feeling disrespected? Or what if we felt confident asking for a raise? It would be game-changing, right? Not to mention, if we could have positive conversations with our colleagues about things they are doing (that drives us nuts), it would significantly improve the quality of our lives at work.

Doesn't this sound like a better option than feeling miserable all of the time? Or worse, having to change jobs?

WHAT IS IT ABOUT THE CONVERSATION THAT FEELS SO DIFFICULT?

Often when we are upset about something someone did or said to us, there are painful feelings at play. We may not consciously be aware of our hurt, frustration, anger, or anxiety. But we feel vulnerable, as our self-worth is at stake, and if we already have low self-esteem, we feel our competence is being judged.

We are often concerned about how others see us. We ask ourselves questions like, "Have I embarrassed myself?" or "Will I come out of this looking like a bad person?"

Our fears can take over, having us feeling scared about our future.

We worry if having a difficult conversation will make the situation worse. We wonder if we will be able to work with this person again, or what effect this will have on our career or livelihood.

When we feel like our relationship (or job) is at risk, or the outcome is uncertain, it may stop us from doing anything, and we accept the current situation. Unfortunately, this may cause us to withdraw and shut down, worsening things for us.

As you can see, keeping these unresolved feelings and fears inside can cause a lot of anxiety and affect our overall mood. So, as difficult as it may be, the best thing to do is prepare to have a difficult conversation.

PREPARING FOR A DIFFICULT CONVERSATION

Rushing into a confrontation or reacting in a situation without thinking things through, usually ends up with negative results. That is why preparation is our friend.

First, we need to recognize with any situation, there are multiple stories at play. These stories come down to our different perspectives.

Family Scenario:

When I was a teenager, I used to work in the family-independent grocery store. One day, my older brother kept pushing me harder and harder. I got so mad at him. I just had it! I remember standing in front of him, and I took my apron off and told him, "I quit!" I admit, not my finest moment. But I was very upset.

I knew my story. My brother pushed me too far. He expected too much out of me. He was harder on me than any of the staff. I worked longer than anyone at the store as well. But my story was missing his perspective.

His story was he wanted me to learn more about the store than anyone else so I could work anywhere. He believed in me and knew he was preparing me for management. At the time, I didn't realize his reasoning. I felt like he was unfair to me.

We can all come up with a list of reasons we feel we were unjustly judged or treated. And we could continue to live with the built-up resentment inside. Or, we can choose to do something about it.

There are three reasons to have a difficult conversation:

- You want to **LEARN** their story.
- You want to **EXPRESS** your views and feelings.
- You want to **SOLVE** the problem together.

If we can stop and think before we react, our relationships would be improved. Doing this would have been a much better way to resolve my story with my brother!

WHAT HAPPENED? WHAT CAUSED THE NEED FOR HAVING A DIFFICULT CONVERSATION?

Second, we need to look at what happened and mentally prepare for the conversation. If we don't, we can escalate the situation.

Think about what happened and ask yourself:

- What is the **TRUTH** of what happened?
- What were the **INTENTIONS** of the people involved?
- Who was **RESPONSIBLE** for the situation?

We will look at truth, intentions, and responsibility to help you prepare for your difficult conversation.

CALM DOWN AND REFLECT SO THAT YOU CAN GET TO THE TRUTH

During a conflict, we can have one of two reactions:

- **Option #1: We can flip out and get angry right away and say things that we later regret.** With this response, we assume we have all the information we need to understand what happened and react. Our goal here is to persuade them we are right and they are wrong. If we are not careful, we may lash out, saying something cruel that we will later regret. This approach usually ends up in a painful conflict.
- **Option #2: We can stop and think about it and come back later when we are calm.** With this response, we have had time to think through some things. We are better able to provide a more thoughtful response. We assume each of us is bringing different information and perceptions to the table. So there are likely to be essential aspects of the situation each of us doesn't know. Therefore, our goal is to explore each other's stories to gain a deeper understanding of the problem (how and why).

QUESTION:

- Which option are you most likely to choose when you are upset?
- Which do you think is the better option?

INTENTIONS

As we look at intentions, it can sometimes bring up strong emotions, as we often assume we already know what they intended.

We don't need to discuss our thoughts on intentions during our conversation, as it can often lead us off in the wrong direction.

If you assume you know what the other person intended and if you believe they were aware of the impact their actions would have on you, then you must be a world-class mind reader or psychic. Neither of these is likely. So, is it possible you don't actually know what they were thinking and what their intentions were?

What's important to share during your difficult conversation is the impact it had on you. You will also learn what they were thinking and the effect you may have had on them.

So, while you may feel like they intended to hurt you, tick you off, or stab you in the back, your goal with the difficult conversation is to let them know how their behaviour impacted you. Not to make assumptions.

By stopping and thinking before we respond, we can provide a thoughtful response that moves us in the direction of a solution.

WHO IS RESPONSIBLE?

It's difficult to admit when we are wrong. Whether it's our pride, ego, or strong desire to protect our reputation, sometimes it feels more comfortable to assume the other person is wrong. So we play the blame game and blame everyone and anyone but ourselves when things go wrong.

When we approach conflict with this mentality, our goals are to get the other person to admit they were wrong, take responsibility, and make amends to us. But this approach does not work. Just because we point the finger at them and say, "You did it!" does not mean they will own it. Also, we can't control other people. We can only control how we react to them. By responding this way to conflict, you are almost sure to push people away.

Another approach is often taken by the type of person who hates conflict and does anything to avoid it. They often take responsibility to move on quickly. This approach is not healthy, and it will leave us feeling like a doormat. We don't want that!

Instead, a thoughtful response to a difficult conversation would assume both parties have probably contributed to this mess. Therefore, it makes sense they both need to work to clean it up. The goal, in this case, would be to understand how the actions of both parties produced this result. By doing this, the other person is more likely to work with you on a win-win solution instead of getting into a defensive mode.

LOOK WITHIN FOR ANSWERS

Self-awareness is key to helping you prepare for your difficult conversation. To prepare your mindset for the conversation, you need to accept the following:

- You will make mistakes
- Your intentions are complex
- You have contributed to the problem

Think back to a recent conflict you have had. How did the conflict start? Were you trying to change the other person? If so, you should realize people do not change unless they want to change. We can't change other people. We can only change our reactions to them. Ask yourself:

- How were you feeling inside?
- Did they attack who you believe yourself to be?
- What were your emotions?
- What was coming up for you?
- Did they attack your values or our identity?
- Is the sense of conflict inside only you?

To demonstrate this point, I want to share a personal story.

When my kids were all living at home, I remember I would blame others for my unhappiness. "If only my daughter would clean her room, or my son didn't come home so late, or my husband listened to me or helped me around the house," then all my problems would be over.

If only I would have learned what I am teaching you now, back then. My regrets would not be so big. There were many poor reactions, but the one saving grace for me was I went and apologized for my behaviour. There was a better way to address the situation, and I blew it.

I am super close with my kids today, and they say it was because I took responsibility for any wrongdoing. We both acknowledged our distasteful reactions and looked at how we could do things better the next time.

Can you relate to my story?

OUR IDENTITY

At our core, we believe (and ask) three things about ourselves:

- Am I competent?
- Am I a good person?
- Am I worthy of love?

Do you consider yourself a great mom, terrific leader, good speaker, and trustworthy employee? If you believed this and someone said something contrary to what you believe about yourself, you are likely to get upset.

When our identity is attacked, we often shut down and withdraw. Having our identity threatened or challenged can be triggering, and brings us back to a time during our childhood or life where we felt attacked or unloved because of who we believed we were.

So when we have our identity attacked as an adult, we are dealing with the current pain and residue of unresolved feelings from earlier in our lives, which can be overwhelming.

This is especially true for women. We may not stand up for ourselves, and when we do, it is seen as unacceptable behaviour, resulting in women getting imposter syndrome and questioning if they belong.

But when we feel our identity is being attacked, we should remember there may be a lot at stake psychologically for both of us. As human beings, we are complex. None of us are perfect. It is our unique identity, and no one can take that away from us.

Our goal is to understand the identity issues on the line for each of us and build a more complex self-image to maintain our balance better.

Client Scenario:

One of my clients received a promotion. Despite being completely qualified and the right pick for the position, she didn't feel it. She felt like she was a fraud and everyone was looking at her and judging her. She believed any moment someone was going to find out and tell her boss she was a fraud.

We worked for several weeks on just her identity, uncovering what she truly believed about herself.

Like with my client, when your identity is attacked, you need to believe in yourself and remember what I said before.... you will make mistakes. And that is okay, as it is the only way you will learn. It's how we all learn.

THE "FEELINGS" CONVERSATION

Some of us do everything to avoid our feelings. We stuff it down with being busy, shopping, social media, food, etc. At the core of all of these vices and "isms" are feelings trying to be denied or suppressed.

Our first reaction to conflict might be it is their fault for hurting our feelings. After all, they should have known better. And anger says, "I am going to show them what it feels like." We may assume, "My feelings are irrelevant, and sharing them wouldn't be helpful to others," or, "My feelings are their fault, and they need to hear about them."[21] And in this type of adverse scenario, our shared goal is to avoid talking about our feelings or let them have it!

However, if we stopped and thought about everything before reacting, we would understand feelings are the heart of the situation. And feelings are incredibly complex.

To understand our feelings, we have to dig down deep to understand what's happening to us. Our feelings may come from a trigger of a previous bad situation. So, what we'd want to do then is to address the feelings (ours and theirs) without judging, blaming, or attributing negative intentions. We need to acknowledge feelings before problem-solving.

Most of the work in a difficult conversation happens after the situation/behaviour and before the difficult conversation. Difficult conversations don't happen at the moment. They occur after we have taken the time to investigate what was *really* going on. That is why we are discussing this crucial preparatory work.

IMPACT VS INTENT

One of the things we also need to do to prepare for a difficult conversation is to look at the impact the behaviour/situation has on us (and others) and the potential reasons for that impact. For example, we need to look at our feelings and ask ourselves open-ended questions such as:

- What's my perspective on this?
- What do I think about this?

---

[21] https://www.mdmunicipal.org/DocumentCenter/View/2607/Difficult-Conversations?bidId=

- What are my intentions?
- How did their behaviour affect me?
- What is my guess about their intentions?
- Could the other person have acted unintentionally?
- How is my behaviour affecting them?
- Does any of this change how I feel?
- What is my purpose for discussing the situation?
- What are my desired results?

Before moving into the actual structure of having a difficult conversation, let's review what we've learned:

- **Contribution** – What did I contribute to the problem? What did they contribute?
- **Feelings** – What feelings underlie my judgments? What might they be feeling?
- **Identity** – How does this situation threaten my identity?

HOW TO HAVE A DIFFICULT CONVERSATION

You have explored what was happening inside of you, and you've done all of the internal work to mentally and emotionally prepare for the difficult conversation. You have also considered what may have been going on for the other side, and you feel confident you have the right attitude for an effective and productive talk. Now we move onto the conversation itself.

To set yourself up for success during your conversation, we will review the following elements of my method for having a difficult conversation:

- Time, Place, Tone
- Third Story

- Listen and Share Feelings
- Invite to Problem Solve

Scenario – Sandy:

One of my clients, Sandy, is a very popular councilwoman in a medium-sized city. She is kind and considerate, and she tries to take the high road in how she interacts with people. Sandy does not get directly angry at people. Instead, she lets it fester when she gets home.

After experiencing a situation at work, which she described as the "straw that broke the camel's back," she called me. Sandy was ready to explode. She didn't sleep well or eat well. Sandy became very cranky with her husband even though he is incredibly supportive. She began to withdraw and shut down, declining coffee dates from friends and no longer taking their dog for walks.

As we chatted, she told me another councilwoman, Janice, was being very passive-aggressive towards Sandy in Council meetings. Whenever Sandy shared an idea or thoughts on a particular proposal, Janice would reply sarcastically. Janice's body language was very harsh, as she would laugh, look at others and roll her eyes, look away when Sandy was talking, and even took her phone out every time Sandy had the floor. Sandy felt her identity was being threatened. She asked, "Am I a good person?" "Am I competent?" "Am I worthy of love and respect?"

She started to feel maybe this line of work wasn't for her. Self-doubt began to creep in as the saboteur on her shoulder was pecking at her constantly. Sandy wanted me to advise her on what to do. She asked, "How can I stand up for myself without making Janice feel defensive right away?

Sandy's situation is perfect for demonstrating how to have a difficult conversation.

TIME, PLACE, TONE

First of all, let's discuss the time, place, and tone: Never confront someone in front of others or during a meeting, as it never ends well. Instead, choose a private place where you can sit down. Select a date and time that works well for both of you (allowing enough time for you to both be heard). Your voice should be calm and friendly, and the tone of the discussion amicable.

Using the scenario with Sandy, I suggested she approach Janice after the meeting ended, and I recommended a way for Sandy to introduce the subject with Janice:

> *"Hey Janice, can I talk to you for a minute? Janice, I have been feeling a little confused lately. I have noticed whenever I have anything to say in council meetings, you seem disinterested. Can we go for coffee down the road? I really want to hear your perspective on this."*

Sandy might meet with some resistance at first. Since Janice is her peer, she may still get defensive and push Sandy further. Most times, though, when you tell someone you want to hear their perspective on something, and especially if you buy them a free coffee, they will agree. After all, an invitation to a coffee date does not seem threatening, where you would attack them.

Here is another example:

> *"Hey Joe. Can I talk to you for a minute? Joe, I have heard a few rumblings from the staff about your driven nature here at the office, and I was hoping we could go for coffee this afternoon at the little cafe down the road." Joe may ask for more information. Remember, you need to talk in a private off-site location, as this is the most non-threatening. Casually say, "I'd rather get out of here for a bit anyway," and leave it there.*

THIRD STORY

And then we move to the third story—or the unbiased version of what happened. Describe the behaviour/situation concretely and specifically, without blaming or negative judgment. Share your point of view as a third person would. The other person should not interrupt. Own your part. Use "I" statements.

Sandy:

"So, Janice, it seems as if you and I may have different perspectives on the ideas I had on the hospital renovation. You seemed angry and irritated. I realize I may have misinterpreted your actions in the meeting, so I really want to hear your thoughts on this. After I hear what you have to say, I will share a bit about what was going on for me. And maybe we can figure something out."

Joe:

"Joe, as I told you earlier, I have heard some grumbling around the office, and I wanted to check in with you. While I know you are driven and want to do a good job, and want your bonus, I have heard you have discouraged others from doing the same, and have at times taken their ideas and used them as your own. I have also heard you take over team meetings and do not allow others to speak. I would really like to hear where you are coming from. What's your take on this?"

LISTEN AND SHARE FEELINGS

Seek first to understand. Listen to the other person with no interruptions. Understand feedback is hard to take. Even the best conflict resolution consultant may find themselves defensive.

Sandy:

Janice didn't quite know how to respond. She didn't say anything in the meeting she was aware of, but Sandy was right. Janice disagreed with the hospital proposal, and she felt angry this proposal was even being discussed.

Sandy said, "I am not here to accuse or judge you. We are both entitled to our feelings on this. Please tell me what was going on for you."

Janice then shared her ideas and talked about her feelings. Janice also told Sandy she had family issues she had been struggling with. Sandy was then happy to share her feelings. She realized her initial thoughts about Janice were not entirely correct. Sandy assumed Janice's actions meant she knew everything going on for Janice. She was wrong.

Joe:

Joe's first reaction was defensive. He denies. You listen.

You say, "Joe, I do want to know how you view these accusations. I am not here to judge you. Perhaps you can give me your side of the story. For example, do you see very many people talking at meetings? And what about Sarah's idea about how to reach out to more clients? You mentioned it in one of your meetings."

Hopefully, with this prompting, Joe might be looking at it from the other perspective, and learn how his actions might be affecting the team. He wasn't intentionally doing these things, but he now admits this did indeed happen.

PROBLEM SOLVE

Many, many times, when you approach a difficult conversation like this, you realize there are no problems at all. About 98% of conflict is miscommunication. Body language and the tone of voice, and the misinterpretation of these critical factors, are often to blame. We will be discussing body language in another chapter.

If there is indeed a problem, remember, this discussion is not only about your perceived disagreements. It is mostly to help identify how you can work together to solve the problem while not disrespecting each other.

This is where you can say something like, "So how can we prevent this from happening again? I do not want us to be on opposite sides where we both dread to go to our meetings." Again, be sure to speak in "I" terms. For example, "I want to ask what you think about it, and then I will tell you what's happening for me. Then let's see where we can go from there."

EVALUATE AFTER A FEW WEEKS

It's a good idea to foster the relationship by checking in to see if you are both okay. I recommended Sandy go back to Janice after a few weeks to check in.

Sandy simply said, "Hey, Janice, let's chat again."

At this time, you ask how things are going. Is she feeling any changes with reactions to her in the last few weeks? If all is good, make a note to talk in a few weeks again.

However, if you think your situation is beyond having a "difficult conversation," please read Chapter seven, where we talk about dealing with angry people and assessing whether it's time to cut the cord on the relationship.

"Sometimes the most important conversations are the most difficult to engage in."

– Jeanne Phillips

IN CONCLUSION

If there is only one thing you learn from this book, I hope it's on how to have a difficult conversation, as I know how pivotal it will be to help you improve your relationships. In the next chapter, we are going to look at passive-aggression. I highly recommend the book *Difficult Conversations*, which goes much deeper than I can.

MINI-DISCLAIMER:

As I am not a mental health professional or counsellor, if you are in an abusive relationship or dealing with an acute crisis situation, I highly recommend you immediately seek professional help.

REFRAME
WHAT YOU NOW KNOW

If you have been allowing negative emotions to fester inside you, you can use this tool to enable you to have a difficult conversation.

As we've seen, blowing up in anger is not the solution. Instead, seek a healthy way to discuss issues, as they foster relationships and help the workplace environment.

Additionally, the beauty of this is when other people in your work start seeing you do this, they start going, "Wow! She is so powerful. She dealt with that beautifully." Respect from the rest of the team is visible. And others start behaving in the same way!

By listening and engaging with a person, you can change how you react. You will mitigate conflict instead of avoiding difficult conversations, which leads to copacetic workplace relationships. You do this, not others.

Once you communicate effectively to others about how their behaviour affects you, you will likely notice 98% of your conflicts are due to a misunderstanding. Your relationships will improve by being willing to listen and really hear the other person's story and then go on to share yours!

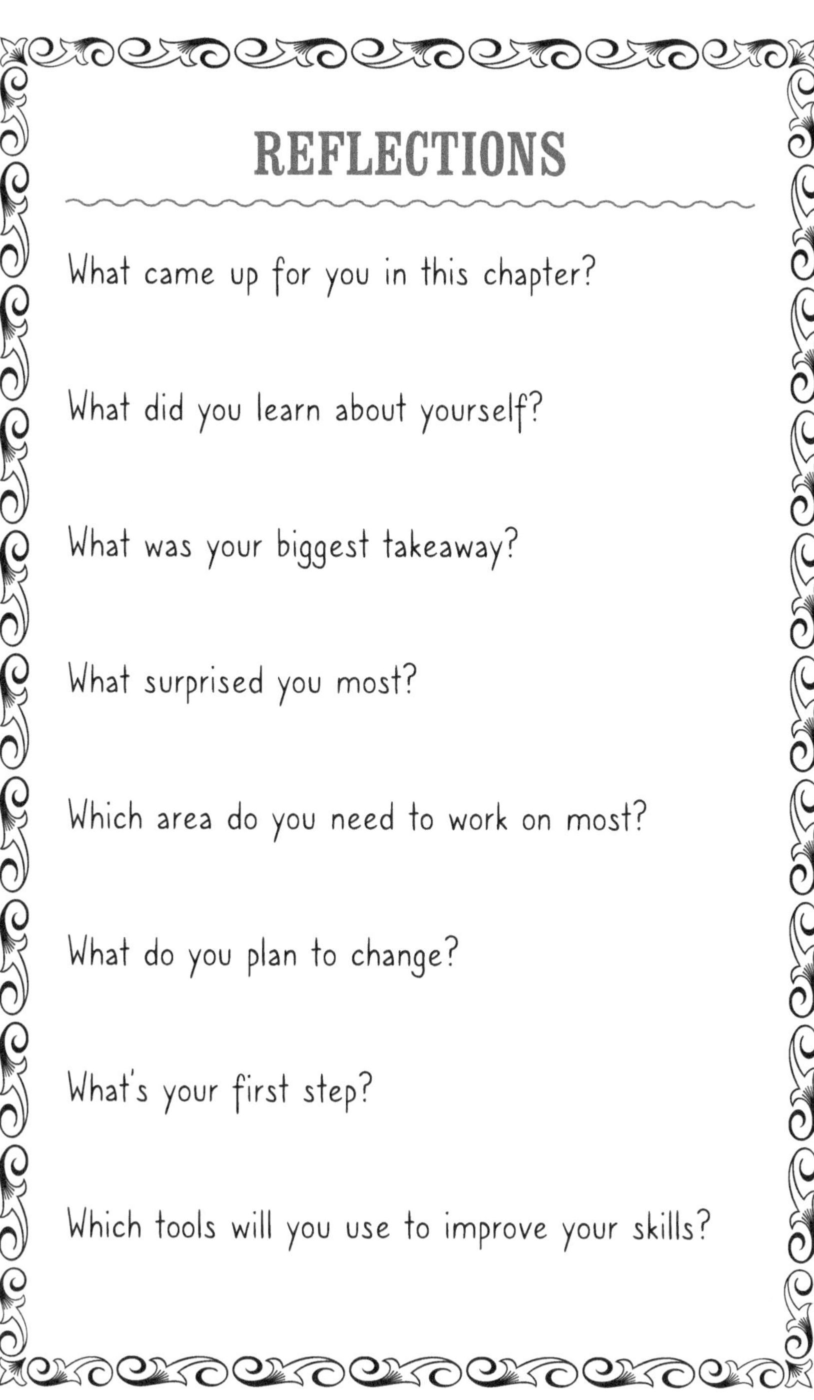

REFLECTIONS

What came up for you in this chapter?

What did you learn about yourself?

What was your biggest takeaway?

What surprised you most?

Which area do you need to work on most?

What do you plan to change?

What's your first step?

Which tools will you use to improve your skills?

CHAPTER SIX

PASSIVE-AGGRESSION

"I'd rather have an enemy who admits that they hate me, than a friend who secretly puts me down."

– Karen Salmansohn

This chapter is going to tackle a difficult subject: passive-aggression. I'm sure we've all experienced people in life who are difficult to deal with. Does this sound familiar?

- A self-absorbed neighbour who seems to take immense joy in rubbing in your nose all of her "new toys"
- Your fall-down-drunk uncle your family never talks about
- A bully colleague who gets away with verbally abusing everyone at work because of his high sales records
- The Avon sales rep who enjoys making snarky, sarcastic remarks
- A partner/spouse who slams dishes around because they are unhappy with something you did or said

- A colleague who is super friendly to you to your face, but you overhear her talk negatively behind your back

Tim Murphy and Loriann Hoff Oberlin, authors of the book, *Overcoming Passive-Aggression,* have influenced my work around conflict management and communication. They have helped me to recognize passive-aggressive behaviours in so many people. And I've been able to call out passive-aggressive behaviour in others and even myself.

With all the research I have done and the years of practicing this with my clients, even I am guilty of the occasional passive-aggressive slip-up. So, please don't fool yourself into believing you are immune to it! Just the other day, I made a snide (passive-aggressive) comment to my husband and caught myself afterwards.

A result of learning about how toxic passive-aggressive behaviour is and how it can be corrected, I've come to realize how massively it can improve relationships. Interestingly enough, when I call out people on passive-aggressive behaviour, I found a lot of it was not intentional. And their behaviour changed as a result of the difficult conversations I had with them. So, there is hope!

On the other hand, you may be reading this book because you have been told YOU are passive-aggressive. For example, your boss said you need to fix your "poor attitude" and "bad behaviour." Or perhaps your colleagues complain you are "mean to them" in meetings. If this is the case, I have provided you with some information on how to correct this type of toxic behaviour.

Either way, this chapter will look at how we can identify and deal with passive-aggression to salvage our relationships while not scapegoating certain people. Not to mention, by doing "the work," the quality of life can be significantly improved for all involved.

As hidden or repressed feelings cause passive-aggression, the most effective way to address the behaviour is to get to the root of the issue.

WHAT IS PASSIVE-AGGRESSIVE?

Passive-aggressive behaviour can be exhibited in one's personal and professional life. Because we know these people personally or professionally, it can be relatively easy to recognize yet incredibly tough to address. This is why it's important to know how to have a difficult conversation (covered in the previous chapter).

HOW TO RECOGNIZE PASSIVE-AGGRESSION IN SOMEONE

Passive-aggression, in the bigger hidden anger picture, can look like some, or all, of the following:[22]

1. Chronic irritability and chronic depression return
2. Self-absorption/narcissism/vanity (an entitlement personality)
3. Low self-esteem, weak boundaries, and family image complexity
4. Self-destructive behaviour or acting out
5. Aggression that gets redirected onto a safer target or a scapegoat
6. Substance abuse and addictive behaviour
7. Social immaturity
8. Unacceptable conduct that is excused for any reason

As you can see, unchecked, passive-aggressive behaviour can be destructive. For friends, family, and coworkers, dealing with passive-aggressive people can be miserable and even painful at times. And for the person suffering from this type of behaviour,

---

[22] Murphy, T. & Hoff Oberlin, L. Overcoming Passive-Aggression: How to Stop Hidden Anger from Spoiling Your Relationships, Career and Happiness. Boston. Da Capo Press. 2005.

it can be isolating, as people may no longer want to communicate or spend time with you. After all, would you want to hang out in a home that had a wrecking ball tearing down the walls and everything in its path?

Because girls are taught to be "nice," it's more common to see passive-aggression in women than in men.

HOW TO KNOW IF YOU ARE PASSIVE-AGGRESSIVE

When I'm working with passive-aggressive clients, I look at areas in their life to help tell a story. How is the client currently doing in life? What happened in their past (e.g., childhood, failed relationships, social problems)?

Although it's unpleasant to have to deal with anger in the workplace, it can serve as a catalyst for positive change and growth. So while our past may have many unpleasant and perhaps painful memories, it has created a behaviour pattern that can be identified and corrected.

For example, if you were not allowed to show your feelings as a child, you may have repressed your angry feelings and taken them out in another way (e.g., breaking toys, being mean to siblings). As an adult, you may have grown up to have a series of broken relationships and failed employment. You can't figure out why you keep getting fired or why none of your ex's will call you back. Sound familiar?

No worries; with an honest look at what's happening for you, we can get to the root cause of what's making you angry.

Following is a list of 30 questions for you to answer. There are no right or wrong answers, just what is true for you. There is also no judgment. My role here is to help you with your hidden feelings so you can recognize what's coming up for you and make healthier choices when engaging with others.

I invite you to use this self-reflection (non-clinical) diagnostic tool to understand why you react the way you do.

HOW ARE THINGS IN YOUR LIFE?

1. What expression of anger was prohibited in your home as a child?
2. Did you, or do you, struggle to please your parents?
3. Did your parents deny or fail to value your fundamental needs and wants?
4. If you were appropriately assertive for yourself, did you feel afraid or punished?
5. Did the attachment to your parents change in any abrupt way or feel threatened?
6. Would you describe your parents as having a negative attitude when you were growing up?
7. Do you take action to protect the status quo rather than try out new approaches?
8. Do you use brief answers or short phrases because you're afraid to speak up?
9. Does your smile disguise your truly frustrated emotions?
10. Do others tell you about an interpersonal problem they think you have that you don't see?
11. Are you ever intentionally slow-performing a request?
12. Do you tell others you don't understand their requests or concerns so they'll leave you alone?
13. When you disagree, do you feel less anxiety by silencing your frustration?
14. Do others feel you have all-or-nothing thinking, often misinterpret a situation, or read things into it?
15. If you see a coworker headed for a big mistake, do you keep quiet?
16. When afraid to share your opinion, do you later resent things not going your way?
17. Do you bristle when others criticize your work?
18. Do you suffer uncomfortable feelings with food, alcohol, drugs, sex, or gambling?

19. Do you often feel the problems you encounter are someone else's fault?
20. Do you continue an argument past its logical end?
21. Does the fear of rejection prevent you from taking action?
22. Do you feel others can make better decisions than you can?
23. Have you ever turned in projects containing errors or omissions that would cause problems for someone?
24. Do you yearn for more freedom in a relationship but at the same time wish to be close?
25. Have you had a hard time following the wishes of those in authority?
26. Do you resent someone telling you how to do a better job?
27. Do you experience a secret glee, and maintain an advantage over others?
28. Do you keep your feelings inside for so long you eventually explode in unexpected outbursts?
29. When a person is too demanding of you, do you look for ways for him to fail?
30. Have you put your foot in someone's path because you resented that person's good fortune?

Figure 8. Murphy, T. & Hoff Oberlin, L. Overcoming Passive-Aggression: How to Stop Hidden Anger from Spoiling Your Relationships, Career and Happiness. Boston. Da Capo Press. 2005.

By answering the questions, you can identify what's coming up for you and why you are experiencing your feelings. It will help us to determine if you are exhibiting passive-aggressive behaviours.

Again, the purpose here is not to give you a definitive score but rather the presence of your own hidden needs, fears, and things you may be avoiding. The more "yes" answers you have tallied, the more you're concealing emotions, including anger. These repressed, angry feelings would render anyone more opt for acting passive-aggressively. It's a reflection of what's happening for you.

MINI-DISCLAIMER:

This tool is by no means an official diagnostic tool that medical professionals use. The advice in this chapter is simply a starting point of discussion for you to have with your healthcare providers, as this book does not provide you with a medically prescribed treatment plan.

ACKNOWLEDGE YOUR ROLE

If you have a passive-aggressive personality, you need to own it and realize your behaviour harms you and everyone around you. If you want to have a life with fulfilling relationships, then it's necessary to take responsibility for your part in fixing the unwanted behaviour. Remember, it does not in any way mean you are a terrible person. Your behaviour needs to be reframed.

If you have a person in your life who portrays passive-aggressive behaviours towards you, I have provided you with tools to use so you can communicate in a non-threatening way to them and will enable them to hear your concerns.

HOW TO OVERCOME PASSIVE-AGGRESSION

Becoming aware of ourselves is the first step in making any changes. Although this is just the first step, it can sometimes be the toughest. Objectively looking at ourselves can bring up painful emotions. It can have us wanting to deny truths because they are too difficult to face.

But truly knowing who we are, what we like and don't like, and what we will and won't tolerate, helps us learn what makes us tick. It helps us uncover our triggers and hidden feelings to deal with them before acting out.

To become self-aware requires a desire to change something about ourselves, which takes great courage. And if you take the step in moving forward, you should feel proud of the work you are about to embark on.

We also need to understand our desire and our "why." For example, if you have struggled to maintain a relationship and would love to get married someday and have a family, this would be a big "why" for you! Or if you have lost several jobs due to your "attitude" and you really want to move into a larger apartment, your "why" would be to get a higher paying job where you can grow and develop as an employee. And if you have struggled to maintain relationships with your family, now would be the time to prioritize fostering these relationships. Again, you have another fantastic "why" to keep you motivated to do the work!

Next, you need to accept that dealing with passive-aggressive behaviour will take work. It will require patience, honesty, and acceptance. You are not a bad person, as passive-aggressiveness is a learned behaviour. If you go back to the 30 questions you answered earlier, you will identify situations that may have caused you to hold in your feelings. It's okay. This book will help you address this and help you to lead a healthy and productive life.

Now we need to look at what's going on inside and the behaviour itself. If you were my client, I would ask you some of the following questions to get to the bottom of what's happening. For example, I need to know if we are looking at communication issues or something more serious, such as passive-aggressive or aggressive behaviour.

Psychology Today recommends we undergo an "unlearning process." This process requires us to "break down the origins of our thoughts, attitudes, behaviours, feelings, and biases."[23] And we'd need to ask ourselves the following unlearning process questions.[24]

---

[23] https://www.psychologytoday.com/us/blog/the-gen-y-psy/202004/the-power-unlearning

[24] https://www.psychologytoday.com/us/blog/the-gen-y-psy/202004/the-power-unlearning

UNLEARNING PROCESS QUESTIONS:

1. Where do these beliefs come from?
2. Do these support my mental health?
3. Is this in alignment with the life I want?
4. Is this congruent with my authenticity and the person I am? The person I want to become?
5. Do I believe this to be true of myself?

As I see clients who are passive-aggressive, I often ask them the following questions to find out how problematic the behaviour is for them.

QUESTIONS I OFTEN ASK MY CLIENTS:

1. What do you see as problematic behaviour?
2. How does it make you feel afterwards?
3. Are you willing to do the work to make improvements in this area?
4. Do you know where your underlying anger is coming from?
5. What is happening in your body when you have these responses?
6. What are some things that happen to you when you are in a passive-aggressive mood?
7. Do you find yourself anxious or depressed?
8. Can you recognize when you start to attack someone verbally?
9. What's going on inside just before it?
10. What are you feeling inside?
11. Do you act the same towards everyone in your life or just some people?
12. Do you recognizeyou have repressed feelings and specifically anger?
13. Who do you want to be?

Figure 9. Douma, Y. (2021). *Reframe: How to Change Your Conversations to Resolve Those Messy Conflicts.*

The next section is to assist you with helping someone else who is passive-aggressive.

DETECTION OF WHEN SOMEONE IS BEING PASSIVE-AGGRESSIVE

To demonstrate how passive-aggressive shows up in everyday attitudes, I have included a list that compares happy versus angry characteristics and attitudes.

While reviewing this list, see if you can identify any answers that are true for you or the people in your life.

ANGRY VERSUS HAPPY CHART

ANGRY	HAPPY
Irritated	Compassionate and empathetic
Impulsive	Patient
Seek immediate gratification	Can delay gratification, require more of self
Demand	Ask
Blast or maintain silence	Openly and calmly discuss
Need to control or obstruct	Want to negotiate, cooperate, resolve problems
Criticize	Respect
Dig in heels	Accept change or differences
Immature, childish	Mature and possessing perspective
Tense, frowns, sighs	Relaxed, smiles, laughs
Blame	Take responsibility
Threaten/punish	Reward/praise
Put down	Inspire
Rely upon rage talk, swearing	Choose more inspiring vocabulary

Figure 10. Murphy, T. & Hoff Oberlin, L.
Overcoming Passive-Aggression: How to Stop Hidden Anger from Spoiling Your Relationships, Career and Happiness.
Boston. Da Capo Press. 2005.

HOW TO "CONFRONT" THIS BEHAVIOUR IN A LOVING WAY

What do you do when someone in your life is exhibiting passive-aggressive behaviour?

I recommend you review the following lists/charts within this chapter to have an understanding of what issue is showing up (for you, them, and different situations), the severity (frequency and intensity), and the toxic impact it's having on your relationships:

- "How Are Things in Your Life" (Figure 8)
- "Questions I Often Ask My Clients" (Figure 9)
- "Angry Versus Happy Chart" (Figure 10)

Now that you have a greater understanding of what's happening and what needs to be resolved, you can make a plan for having a difficult conversation, as discussed in Chapter five.

Next, you will want to have a difficult conversation with them. It is not a finger-pointing type of talk, but rather an opportunity for you to uncover what feelings they may be secretly hiding, causing them to act out. You need to acknowledge their behaviour with you. You will want to make sure you are heard regarding unwanted behaviour. They also need to be heard.

They must understand your intention for this discussion is not to shame them, but instead to help them. Therefore, your delivery must be gentle. It's important to share your purpose of not wanting to cause them more distress, but rather you want to problem-solve together to ensure it doesn't happen again.

We want to acknowledge your intention and then basically solve the problem together and ensure this won't happen again. Remember, the purpose is to help them, not to blame or shame them.

You first need to confront the behaviour in a non-threatening or judgmental way. For example:

- I noticed you are doing …
- I know you are likely not doing this on purpose …

A workplace example might look like this:

- I know you are not missing our project deadline on purpose. So how can I help you? Where is this coming from? What is the root cause?
- What's going on for you? I noticed you slammed your phone down earlier.

Your purpose here is to listen to them. Then offer some help. For example, you could ask:

- Tell me, how can I help you?

In a personal relationship, it may look like this:

- I'm trying to understand what happened. I feel like there's something else underneath the surface that may be bothering you. Our relationship is important to me, but I think something is going on with you. Can you help me to understand?

By asking them compassionate probing questions, you will uncover what is really going on for them. Sometimes people need to be validated to help calm them down.

At this point, you want confirmation their intent was not to tick you off. You will need to acknowledge the person has passive-aggressive behaviours, and help them find alternative ways of communicating with you going forward.

Remember, most passive-aggressive people have been like this their entire adult life, so their tendencies will *not* go away after one difficult conversation. You will need to check in with each other to ensure things are okay and follow up if there is a repeat incident.

Your role in this relationship is to be a collaborator, helping them to uncover their behaviour. You can only do this if you are compassionate and extend grace to them, as they have been uncomfortable with sharing their anger with you or anyone.

Again, no blaming or finger-pointing. Just the intention of helping them from a place of love and care.

"It's easy to remember only the good parts of people if you never see them. Real people are much more complicated."

– Cynthia Lord

IN CONCLUSION

This chapter provided you with some tools to recognize passive-aggression, whether in yourself or those around you. It's important to realize it's possible to overcome this toxic personality trait, as it is a learned behaviour. I have also provided you with some tools to confront the behaviour lovingly to grow your relationship. In the next chapter, we are looking at how to deal with angry (aggressive) people.

REFRAME WHAT YOU NOW KNOW

As passive-aggression is a learned behaviour, it can be unlearned. But it will take more than willpower or a strong "why" to make it happen.

A plan of action and some form of self-monitoring will be needed to stay on top of it. Self-monitoring would include triggers and behaviours.

If we have a passive-aggressive personality, we need to strip away our beliefs and how we act, behave, and live that have been problematic. We were raised with these beliefs taught to us by our parents, elders, society, and the media. All of these are powerful forces in our lives, so it's essential to uncover the root cause, have the will to change, and a process for tracking our progress.

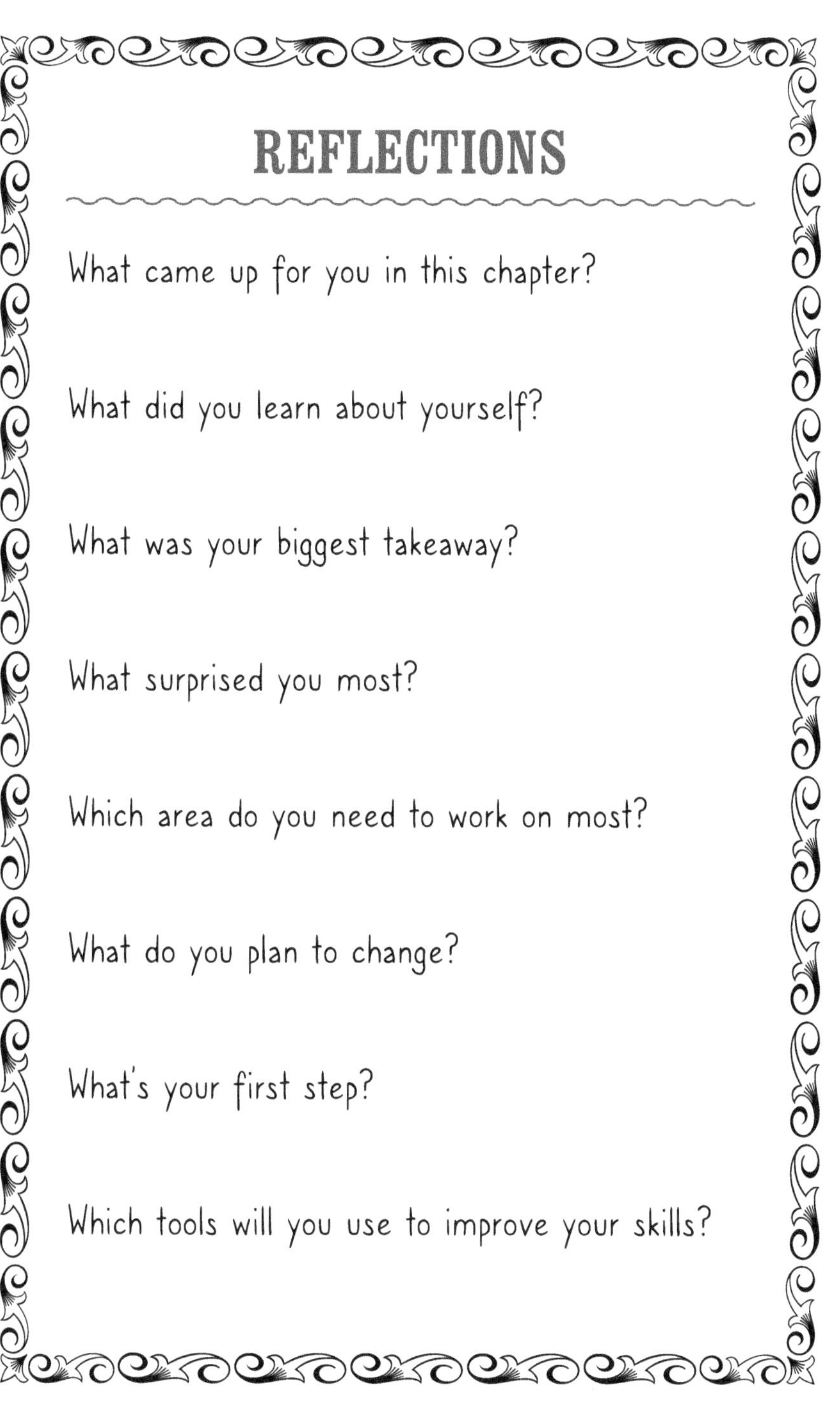

REFLECTIONS

What came up for you in this chapter?

What did you learn about yourself?

What was your biggest takeaway?

What surprised you most?

Which area do you need to work on most?

What do you plan to change?

What's your first step?

Which tools will you use to improve your skills?

CHAPTER SEVEN

DEALING WITH ANGRY PEOPLE

"Angry people are not beautiful."

– Andie MacDowell

So far in this book, we have learned how to have difficult conversations, how to work with different communication styles, and how to confront someone who is passive-aggressive. All of this has provided us with a foundation so we can address angry and, more specifically, aggressive people, as they are much more difficult to work with.

This chapter will provide you with some conflict mitigation tools so you can take care of yourself. However, no matter how much we try to mitigate the situation, some angry people are extremely difficult and often painful to deal with.

Let's face it, no matter how many difficult conversations or conflict management tools we employ, the fact is some people don't play nice in the sandbox! And at some point, we may need to evaluate how healthy it is for us to remain in relationships with certain people. After all, you can be as intentional as you want with people. But if you are communicating to the *wrong* people, the effort will be all for naught.

I'm sure at some point in time, you had "friends" who made you feel bad about yourself, and eventually, you ended your friendship for sanity's sake. Well, after reading this book, and doing a lot of reflection and journaling, you may realize the cost to keep some people in your life is too high. You may decide to weed out angry and toxic folks to make room for people who help you be your best self. It's entirely possible. But let's not get ahead of ourselves quite yet!

MINI-DISCLAIMER:

If you are dealing with anger, harassment, bullying, or aggression, you need to remove yourself from this threatening position. If it's taking place at work, contact your human resources representative. If it is happening in your personal life, reach out to someone for help. If you are in physical harm, contact the police immediately.

WORDS MATTER

I want to share a parable with you that outlines the power of words. The words we say to others and the words they say to us matter. If you are dealing with an angry person, words exchanged are often cruel and intended to cause pain. There are different versions of this parable involving an old, wise man and a feather pillow. Regardless, the lesson is the same: our words matter, and they can stay with someone for their entire life.

In my version, there is a wise grandfather and his grandson.

The grandson was upset about someone at school. He told his grandfather he got so upset he called the boy several bad names.

He admitted being mean to the other boy, and said the other kids were laughing. The grandson admitted he now felt terrible about what he said to the other boy. The grandfather said, "I can understand why you would feel bad. Those words are not very nice things to say to someone." The grandson asked, "Do you think God and the other boy will forgive me?"

A few minutes later, they walked up a steep hill together, carrying a feather pillow. Grandpa told his grandson to open the zipper and release all the feathers. His grandson asked why he was telling him to do this. Grandpa then told him to find every single feather and put it back inside the pillow. The grandson gasped and said, "That's impossible! They've all flown away. I can't find them all!"

The grandfather turned to his grandson and said, "Those feathers are like cruel words we say to other people. Once you say it, you can't take it back. Those words you said to the other boy will remain with him for the rest of his life. Always remember the power words have on others." What should the grandson now do with his classmate?

WHAT DOES AN ANGRY PERSON LOOK LIKE?

Angry people come in all shapes and sizes. If it's someone close to us, we may be used to minimizing and excusing their bad behaviour. But the reality is angry people can resemble or behave like any of the following:

HOW TO IDENTIFY AN ANGRY PERSON:

1. They are mean and intentionally cruel
2. They say mean things
3. They intentionally do things to hurt people

4. They are tense and uptight
5. They have physiological symptoms (e.g., sweating, clenched teeth, veins bulging out of their neck)
6. They don't participate in fun unless it's making fun of others
7. They don't care what people think of them
8. They say whatever is on their mind
9. They appear to be irritated and agitated
10. They are quick to rise emotionally (hot temper)
11. They are unwilling to listen
12. They know everything
13. They throw things or punch things
14. They do not behave rationally

Of course, this list does not describe every angry person. Some people may have other behaviours they typically exhibit, for example, withdraw from others, do not participate in discussions, or become depressed.

Also, consider the passive-aggressive person whose behaviour may appear "nice," but underneath is a burning furnace of hell, as outlined in the previous chapter.

MINI-DISCLAIMER:

As I am not a mental health professional or counsellor, if you are in an abusive relationship or dealing with an acute crisis situation, I highly recommend you immediately seek professional help.

REACTING WHEN YOU DON'T HAVE TIME TO PREPARE

Often people take their anger out on anyone that stands in their way or gets caught in the crossfire. So, you don't have time to mentally prepare for the angry verbal attack.

First of all, when you do not have the luxury of preparing for a conflict, you can still respond to angry people by asking questions to really get to the bottom of their anger.

You can take the high road in these situations by grounding yourself and remember you are okay. Nothing they say can make you lose your confidence. You can have a general plan on how to respond to conflict in general. Others attack when they are all out of options.

Instead of becoming defensive or angry, a subtle strategy to use is to get the other person to explain themselves by asking probing questions:

PRESSURE-RELIEF QUESTIONS:

1. Hey, wait a minute. What's going on? How can I help you?
2. Why would you say that?
3. Tell me more about that.
4. Can you give me an example?
5. What are you really saying?
6. Why would you call me out like that?
7. What about this is important to you?
8. What part do you think I played in this?

Asking these questions takes the pressure off you to answer silly questions or attacks, and puts the onus right back on the aggressor. They then must explain themselves, which is harder to do than lash out. These questions are an excellent tool when you need to calm someone down and get them to really think.

Remember, these types of questions could be used on yourself when your temper gets a bit hot. So think twice before sending an email when you are angry! When you are upset, your words come very quickly to you, and you may push "send" without even thinking about the consequences. You might send your angry email and expect them to come back defensive, so you get ready to pounce on them! You have all of your facts. Or so you thought.

But then the other person comes back and says, "Why would you ask me this?" Or "What part do you think I played in this?" Gee, well, now you have to explain yourself even more. Do you really believe your colleague would do what you accused them of? You now have to go back to this person, eat humble pie, and apologize for assuming they did something wrong. It's best to wait a day before sending it!

Or let's consider the following scenario:

Hillary lost an account because Danielle went behind Hillary's back and talked to Hilary's potential client. Danielle deliberately reached out to the client because it was large, and she needed it to get past her current bonus structure. Danielle got the account, and Hilary was furious. On top of losing the client, Hilary also lost her chance at her next bonus by just a few thousand dollars. This bonus was $10,000! After she realized she had been ambushed, she stormed into Danielle's office.

Hillary: *Who do you think you are? I can't believe what you did. What kind of stupid games are you playing? Not only is my reputation damaged by the crap you said to our clients, but you screwed me out of my bonus that I needed to pay for my daughter's college tuition. I can't believe this! You better watch yourself, girl.*

***Danielle**: I don't know why you are so upset. All I did was tell them of the problems that I was foreseeing with the account. I wasn't trying to throw you under the bus. We had a good rapport, so they said they wanted to work with me. I didn't try to steal them from you.*

***Hillary**: That's a load of garbage, and you know it. You've been eyeing this account for a while now. I know you. I even saw you made changes to their account file without my authority. Who does that? I thought we were supposed to be team players. This was dirty and disgusting. Don't for one second believe this is over. Watch your back, because you don't know who you messed with!! You have been warned.*

This is ugly. And unfortunately, similar situations often happen in the workplace. So how could this be resolved?

Danielle is obviously in the wrong here. She starts to defend her actions, which does not play out well. She denies she intentionally sabotaged Hillary, which she clearly did. She reflects all responsibility in this situation. This is typical in these types of conflicts.

So what now? How can these two diffuse this situation?

Danielle clearly needs to acknowledge the wrong that happened, and sincerely apologize. When someone harms someone else, the only thing left is to apologize. If this does not occur appropriately, Hillary needs to calm down and talk to either the HR department, her direct report, or another safe person to help her calm down. Hillary is losing sleep, she cannot eat, she feels sick, and her migraines are back. This relationship may be damaged beyond repair.

SOLUTION

Let's look at this from another perspective. Who is really in control here? Hillary. She is the one that blew up. Don't get me wrong, as she had every right to become super angry. However, what about if she went about this in a different way?

Instead of coming full on to Danielle as soon as she figured out the deception, Hillary could have held her reaction in and slept on it. She knew she was right, but flipping out in anger would have been disastrous, as the above scenario clearly showed. What else could Hillary have done? I would recommend to Hillary she think about how she could come out looking better. For example, she could have slept on it and gone to the office the next day.

Hillary had options. She could have:

- Asked Danielle to meet in a private place to discuss what went down.
- Asked Danielle to explain things from her perspective.
- Explained how she saw it.
- Asked Danielle how they should solve this.
- Recommended they talk to the boss together.
- Gone to the boss and shared the situation together. Hillary was out $10,000, and Danielle made her bonus. How do you think the boss would have reacted? Maybe at the end of the day, with some adjustments, Hillary would receive her bonus anyway. Perhaps if Hillary discusses this in a calm matter, everything would fall into place. What do you think?

MINI-DISCLAIMER:

As I am not a human resources manager or mental health professional, if you are experiencing violence or harassment in the workplace, contact the proper authorities or healthcare professionals immediately.

ASSESSING THE RELATIONSHIP

As I mentioned earlier, at some point, we need to seriously consider whether it's worth it or not to keep an angry person in our life. Using the following questions, assess the relationship or situation to see if it's worth it.

POTENTIAL REASONS TO RELEASE SOMEONE FROM YOUR LIFE

- Are they unwilling to look at their stuff and work on it?
- Are they causing you too much pain?
- Are they getting in the way of you achieving your hopes and dreams?
- Are they disrupting your life?
- Are they killing you inside?

You may find you have valid reasons to keep someone around (e.g., if it's a boss, coworker, or relative). But if diffusing the situation or using strategies doesn't work, it may be time to sever ties with them.

SALVAGING YOUR RELATIONSHIP WITH AN ANGRY PERSON MAY BE POSSIBLE

- What do they mean to you?
- Are they worth it?
- Will they listen to you and consider your feelings?
- Do you believe you have the empathy, compassion, and patience to help them face their truth and become what you need/want?
- Are you safe in this relationship?

Exiting a healthy relationship can be challenging, but leaving a toxic relationship is especially difficult. Ensure you have the support, and reach out to a professional (e.g., therapist, physician, police) if necessary. The goal is to stay safe during the process.

WHEN YOU'VE EXHAUSTED ALL STRATEGIES...

You've tried difficult conversation. You've tried everything. But after you've done all of that, the person is unchanged, and conflict remains. Therefore, your approach must change.

These are tools to reframe how to approach. It's not going to work all of the time. There are some people out there who are simply jerks. And nothing you do is going to help them.

Counsellors are there to help people with personality disorders, and hopefully they will get professional help.

Conflict is one aspect of leadership development. In my leadership roles, I've had to fire people because they were not willing to work within a specific environment. It's not okay to yell. It's not okay to slam doors. It's not okay to scream in my face. It's not okay to disrespect me. And it's not okay to call me names.

So if this is happening, you need to remove yourself from this threatening situation. If the angry person is your boss, the time may come when you will need to leave the company (if after dealing with HR). If it's someone who works under you, you can work with them to remedy their behaviour. You can tell HR you have repeatedly spoken with the other person regarding the problem, but their behaviour hasn't changed. HR or their boss may decide to fire them or send them for skills training. Or they may send you for counselling or leadership coaching so you can learn techniques to better deal with problematic people.

A choice needs to be made. What are you willing to live with? Can you ignore it long enough? Can you pretend it's not going on?

At some point, you might need to say, "I can't; I'm not going to do this anymore," and make the decision to leave for your own safety, and your own mental and physical health.

"When someone has a sharply different point of view than your own, it's natural to want to either avoid talking to them or to try to convince them they are wrong. But neither is a productive approach."

– Harvard Business Review

IN CONCLUSION

In this chapter, we looked at how serious and potentially dangerous it can be to work with angry, aggressive people. It's important you can recognize an angry person and learn the necessary skills to diffuse the situation as best as you can. Consider if you may need to cut ties with toxic people in your life, to maintain your health and wellbeing. If the toxic person in your life is a colleague, and you've been unsuccessful at having difficult conversations with them, you may consider a job change.

In the next chapter, we will look at some quick and easy tips for maintaining positive relationships.

REFRAME WHAT YOU NOW KNOW

I hope you can recognize what angry people look and behave like, and know how to diffuse the situation using the tools provided in this chapter.

Have you thought about how you would react to an angry person, or how you can get someone to give you an honest answer?

Have you considered if *you* have anger issues? What are your relationships like with your parents, your partner, your colleagues, and your neighbours? What about going back to your childhood—did you get along with your friends and teachers?

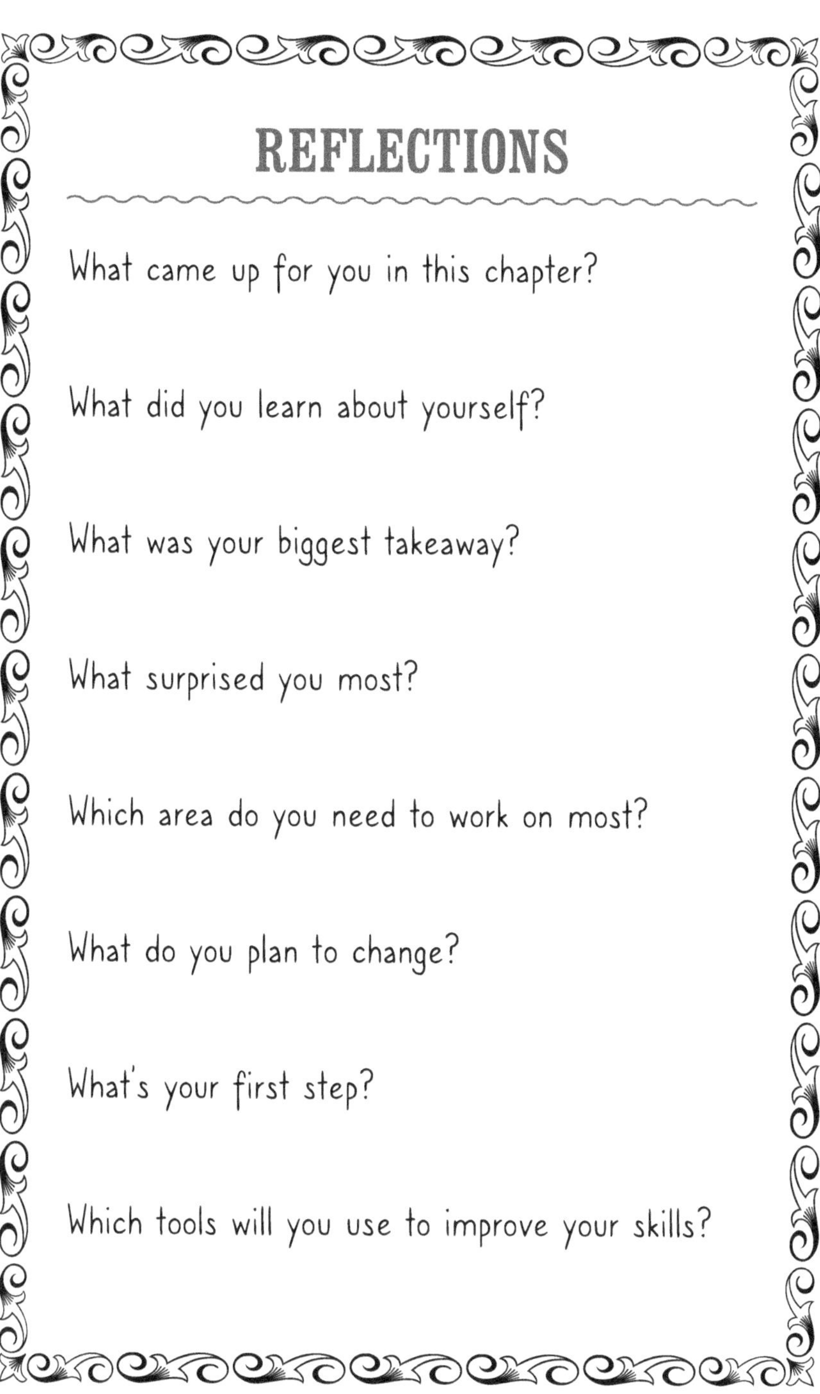

REFLECTIONS

What came up for you in this chapter?

What did you learn about yourself?

What was your biggest takeaway?

What surprised you most?

Which area do you need to work on most?

What do you plan to change?

What's your first step?

Which tools will you use to improve your skills?

CHAPTER EIGHT

QUICK TIPS FOR MAINTAINING POSITIVE RELATIONSHIPS

"I think honest communication, no matter where it comes from, is positive for a relationship."

– Ron White

Scenario:

I had one client who spent most of her days in distress. There was one person in the office who had what some call "a resting bitchy face." She didn't smile a lot, and allowed the frown to stay on her face during most of the day. April, who was a bright and bubbly person, was extremely offended. Why was Michelle always ticked off at her? I recommended she have a conversation with Michelle and tell her how she felt, which she did. Ultimately, April found out Michelle was not upset at all. She was concentrating. I did manage to have a conversation with Michelle, reminding her she might have to put in a little extra effort to say good morning and smile a bit more when around others. Michelle agreed. She did not want others to feel hurt for something that was not at all intentional.

In this chapter, we will look at some common reasons that create miscommunication. I'll provide you with some tools and techniques to help foster your relationships through effective communication.

BODY LANGUAGE

As you can see, it's possible to confuse what someone is saying to us by something as simple as a facial expression. The problem is, we can't read minds. Like Michelle, we assume we know what the other person is thinking, only to find out we were completely wrong!

Why? Well, only 7% of our communication comes from our words. Think about that. Only 7%! Can you think of a time you were confused about one of your colleague's reactions to your words, and thought, "What did I do? Why was she so offended?"

Body language accounts for 55% of the overall message, and the tone of voice accounts for another 38%, leaving only 7% for the words we choose to speak. Shocking, I know! So, despite speaking kindly, if your arms are crossed, or you have a stern look on your face, you are sending signals to other people you may not intend.

EXAMPLES OF BODY LANGUAGE:

1. Rolling your eyes – disrespect
2. Stomping your foot – anger
3. Folding your arms across your chest – defensive
4. Getting in someone's space (standing 2" from someone's face) – control
5. Whistling – boredom
6. Tapping your fingers on the table – impatience

7. Sighing – discouragement
8. Turning your back – disrespect
9. Lack of eye contact – insecurity
10. Direct eye contact – confidence
11. Nervous twitch – anxiety
12. Looking down at phone – boredom, disrespect, not interested
13. Hand gestures – good or bad feelings
14. Furrowed brow – anger or questioning
15. Facial expressions – good or bad feelings

DO NOT EXPECT PEOPLE TO READ YOUR MIND

Sometimes what we *do NOT say* can cause problems in our relationships, as demonstrated in this scenario:

> *Jessica and Bobby got in a fight over whose turn it was to do the dishes. She detested doing the dishes, mostly because she did most of the cooking. Jessica was so frustrated she stormed out of their apartment to go for a drive to calm down.*
>
> *Bobby was very ticked off, as he hated it when Jessica would run off and not tell him where she was going. What if she had a car accident? He was worried.*
>
> *Jessica drove around for a while and listened to some upbeat music. She could understand Bobby's point of view, so she returned home to apologize. But Bobby was so worried about where Jessica had gone to (and ticked off she didn't bother to call him), he blew up at her as soon as she walked through the door. "You're so irresponsible. I can't stand it. What is wrong with you?"*

Separating ourselves from a difficult situation to calm down and gather our thoughts is a great idea. However, we must communicate with the other person to tell them where we are going and when we will be back after we've had some time to calm down. If Jessica had communicated to Bobby she was going for a drive to calm down, he would have also had time to calm down, and they could have hugged and kissed it out when she returned.

OUR EMOTIONS

Our emotions have everything to do with everything. A whole book—or 10, 100, or 1000—still wouldn't be enough to help us understand our emotions. So here, I will touch on this briefly.

Sometimes everyday conversations can get away from us and quickly escalate into an argument. Yet we're unclear as to how this happened. There could be several factors. We know body language and tone can contribute, but how we feel and how well we listen can also affect our ability to communicate effectively.

Another thing to consider is our emotions going into a conversation. We need to consider if we are upset about something else that happened. If so, the other person could pick up on our emotions and react to the "signal" (e.g., frustrating, worried, etc.) we are sending. Therefore, it's best to remain grounded when engaging with others. A few deep breaths and taking some time to collect our thoughts will help us stay calm and collected. When getting over an argument, it's important to acknowledge our anger and not dwell on the situation.

At this point, I want to remind you how stopping from responding or reacting right away is the BEST way of keeping your emotions in check. Always. You also may look into becoming more aware of your emotions, why they are there, and how you can manage them, as discussed in Chapter two on emotional intelligence.

S-TLC MODEL

An alternative technique to help us prepare to have a difficult conversation is the **S-TLC model**, which is short for **stop, think, listen, communicate**. I will explain each point below.[25]

STOP:

When you are aware there is a conflict, take some time to calm down and reflect on the situation. This way, you will be able to return with a proactive stance instead of a reactive stance (if you had stayed in the situation). Remember, someone's anger does not necessarily mean you are the object of another person's anger. So breathe in deeply. Tell yourself not to react. This can be done in mere seconds or over a period of time.

THINK:

Now is the time to think about everything so you can make the best decisions. You can even use "whoa, what's happening" or "tell me more" to give you more time to think about how best to react.

First, you want to think about if you had anything to do with this situation, which will enable you to think more clearly, what caused the conflict, and consider some possible outcomes, such as:

- Doing nothing about the situation (but this is NOT usually very effective in resolving things).
- Changing the other person to suit our needs (but you can't change others).
- Changing yourself – Adapt to the situation or adopt new interests, beliefs, or actions because of something you did differently.

---

[25] Cahn, D. D. & Abigail, R.A. *Managing Conflict Through Communication, 5th Edition*. New York. Pearson Publisher. 2014

- Changing the situation – Look at changing the environment (e.g., moving, leaving a job) or relationship (e.g., ending a friendship or breaking up with a partner). These can often be drastic, life-changing solutions.

Next, think about your goals:

- Instrumental goals – You require action from the other person to remove an obstacle that is blocking you from completing a task.
- Rational goals – You attempt to gain power and establish trust in the relationship with the other person.
- Identity goals – Consider how both parties see each other and do not attack the image or reputation of the other person during the conflict.
- Process goals – Look for alternative ways to manage the communication. Try to use open, fair communication that builds trust and consensus. Holding in your feelings to maintain control and "win" every argument is not a winning solution.

LISTEN:

Now that you have taken some time to think about everything, it's time to communicate with the other person. It's very important to focus on the other person. Even if listening is not a natural skill for you, it's important to hear what they say. Try to remain calm and do not become defensive even if it seems the other person is attacking you.

COMMUNICATE:

Consider the possible ways to respond to conflict. Assertive—not aggressive—communication is best. Once you have heard the other person speak, you can share your thoughts and feelings without attacking them. Remember, effective communication does not infringe on other's interests, concerns, or rights.

If you are unsure about how you express yourself, revisit the chapter on difficult conversations.

With any type of conflict resolution, there is a process to follow. Here is an alternative to the S-TLC model. This six-step confrontation process is easy to remember and can be used when dealing with a difficult conversation.[26]

SIX-STEP CONFRONTATION PROCESS

1. **Preparation** – Identify your problems/needs/issues, pay attention to your self-talk and verbalizing inner messages, visualize and imagine the interaction, and consider what you might say and what the other person might say.
2. **Book the conversation** – Make arrangements for a time and place to meet with the other person.
3. **Interpersonal confrontation** – Now it's time to talk to the other person about your issue.
4. **Consider your partner's point of view** – Demonstrate empathy and consider their beliefs or feelings. Try to put yourself in their shoes. You do not want to be apprehensive about what the other person is saying.
5. **Resolve the problem** – Come to a mutually satisfying agreement with the other person.
6. **Follow up on the solution** – Set a time and limit to reassess the situation.

---

[26] Cahn, D. D. & Abigail, R.A. *Managing Conflict Through Communication, 5th Edition.* New York. Pearson Publisher. 2014

HOW TO GET THE OTHER PERSON TO GIVE YOU AN HONEST ANSWER

Has anyone watched *Columbo?* I know this "dates me," but he gives excellent examples of getting the truth out of people. I highly recommend you watch some old YouTube versions of it.

When questioning potential suspects and people of interest, Detective Columbo would seem to befriend them, speaking with them casually. He would come across as harmless, as he was poorly dressed and would often appear confused, putting the other person at ease. Yet Columbo was clever by using different strategies to get the truth out of the suspect:

1. **He would phrase his question indirectly** by talking about an experience he had or something he liked.
2. **He would appear confused.** If a suspect said something inconsistent or conflicting, he would rub his head and say, "I noticed yesterday you said one thing, and now you are saying something else. I'm confused." He would say things like, "Could you help me understand?" By taking responsibility for the confusion, he disarmed the other person. This tactic enabled them to feel comfortable sharing information with him. Columbo did not accuse or blame them of anything. Instead, he presented the conflicting facts and gave the other person the benefit of the doubt, and when the time was right, he asked clarifying questions.[27]
3. **He would ask one last thing** just before leaving, when the suspect was looking forward to being left alone, and their defences were down. He would turn and ask them a question that would throw them off. Using this "gotcha"

---

[27] https://m.smallbusinessadvocate.com/small-business-article/how-to-confront-liars-using-the-columbo-method

> technique, he caught them off guard and would end up answering the question without overthinking about it. They were just happy he was leaving.[28]

The second tactic Columbo used is a brilliant way to confront someone who is not being honest with you. When you appear to be the one who is confused by the facts and choose not to blame or accuse them, you reduce the chances they will become defensive or mentally check out from the conversation. You could say something like, "I'm sorry, I'm confused about…." "Am I missing something?" They will be more likely to open up and answer your questions, and you will be able to maintain a positive relationship.

ACTIVE LISTENING

You may think you are a good listener, but in reality, most of us are often busy thinking of what we want to say next instead of *truly listening* to the person who is speaking.

Listening with the intent to respond is actually only half-listening. Therefore, we need to listen to them speak to *really understand* where they are coming from. So often, after we listen to their story, we find the conflict ends at this point.

SOME TIPS FOR ENGAGING IN ACTIVE COMMUNICATION:

- Acknowledge content by paraphrasing their message. When you summarize or paraphrase another's communication, they feel you have heard them and understand them.

---

[28] http://changingminds.org/techniques/questioning/columbo_technique.htm

- Acknowledge their feelings to demonstrate you understand. This is so important because feelings are at the heart of every conflict.
- Ask open-ended questions (not questions that require a "yes" or "no" answer). You can say, "Tell me more about this," or "Can you give me an example?" Or even, "Why is this so important to you?"
- Acknowledge your limitations and actions. You can acknowledge your actions if you had any part to play.
- Apologize if appropriate, as it goes such a long way. Make sure there are no "buts" in your apology.
- Commit to change if appropriate. If you need to change because the other person sees a pattern in you, listen to their advice. Ask others if they see the same, and change if you believe it is a real hindrance to your personality. Sometimes we hear things we do not like to hear, but often what we NEED to hear.

SPEAK IN "I" STATEMENTS

Another technique for effective communication is using "I" statements. Using "I" statements allows us to focus on our feelings or beliefs rather than thoughts and characteristics we attribute to the other person. The goal is to recognize the situation and inquire as to what they are specifically upset about, to do better next time. Some examples include:

- "I feel *confused* when I give you a deadline, and it's not completed on time. Is everything okay?"
- "I felt *concerned* when you didn't speak in the meeting. Is everything okay?"

- "I was *hurt and taken aback* when you presented my idea as yours. Was that intentional?"
- "That really *frustrated* me. Was that your intention?"

When you stop pointing fingers at other people and allow them to see you are vulnerable with them, they feel like we have disarmed them.

INTENTIONS VS IMPACT

Let's talk about intentions and impact. Often, we get offended by what a person says because we believe they meant to hurt us. I get this quite often with my husband! He will say something to me I felt was negative, and I often will conclude he meant to hurt me. Thankfully, I have learned how to react now by saying, "I feel you were making fun of me when I told you I had a rough day at work today." Nine times out of ten, it comes down to that silly little thing called body language!

We need to find out all the information before making a judgment. In other words, do not freak out without knowing all the circumstances. Examples of this:

- When you asked the question, "What did I do all day?" it made me feel like you thought I didn't do anything today. Was this your intention?
- When you went to Susan to get her help with this big project, it made me feel I was not good enough. Was this your intention?

More often than not, you will likely find out it was not their intention to hurt you. When you inquire with them, you will realize your thoughts (and assumptions) can sabotage your relationships. So rather than stuff your feelings, it would be best if you talked to others as soon as you can to avoid the hurt feelings and begin to understand the other person better.

LANGUAGE TO USE

We have already talked about this in the Difficult Conversations chapter, but here is a brief recap of the language to use during a conflict.

To *recognize a potential conflict situation*, you could say things like:

- I get the feeling you didn't like what I just said.
- I feel like you may have been offended by what I said in the meeting.
- I get the sense what I said was hurtful to you.

Next, you want to *demonstrate compassion* and feel them out:

- I'm sorry. I didn't mean to hurt your feelings.
- I'm sorry it made you feel like that. This was not my intention.

If you are getting upset by something someone says to you:

You want to speak to them calmly and respectfully so you do not escalate the situation.

For example, if your colleague Joe has been rude to you in staff meetings and embarrassing you, you can ask him to join you for coffee. Tell him you value your working relationship and want to discuss something on your mind.

During coffee, tell Jack you have been uncomfortable by some things he said about you. Ask him what his thoughts were. As you're listening, find out his intention, as you do not want to base his behaviour on your *assumptions*.

Listen to him first *before* you respond. You may find he was unaware, and he is apologetic. Or you may find he has been upset with you about something and was too afraid to tell you. You never know unless you ask. Remember you don't have to like him, but you need to respect each other in the workplace.

NO "BUT'S"!

Have you ever argued with someone, and it looks like they tried to listen to you. They even apologized to you. And then the dreaded "BUT" comes out of their mouths! NOOO! The word "but" following an apology often negates the apology. Synonyms for the word "but" are "nonetheless," "nevertheless," "even so," "still," and more. You get the idea. The word "but" negates any apology that came before it. How often do you use the word "but" in your arguments?

For example,

- "I'm really sorry I hurt your feelings, but I was feeling pretty crappy"
- "I'm sorry I'm late for the meeting, but traffic was insane. Nevertheless, I'm here now. What did I miss?"
- "I'm sorry I didn't call you back right away, but it looks like the issue has been resolved now anyway."

BOUNDARIES

Maintaining boundaries is very important for maintaining healthy, respectful relationships. Following are five types of boundaries to be mindful of:[29]

- **Emotional** – boundaries around inappropriate topics, emotional dumping, and dismissing emotions.

[29] https://www.facebook.com/164173260604347/photos/a.1218482688506727/1258059581215704/

- **Mental** – freedom to have your own thoughts, beliefs, values, and opinions.
- **Physical** – proximity, touch, unwanted comments regarding appearance or sexuality.
- **Material** – boundaries around possessions, when they can be used and how they are treated.
- **Time/Energy** – boundaries around time, lateness, when to contact, favours, and free labour.

HOW TO CALM YOUR ANGER

Anger has a way of taking over when we get upset. Fight or flight anger is our "primitive survival brain" taking over. Following are some techniques that will help prevent us from getting to a Level 10 on the anger scale (0=calm; 10=furious):[30]

- **Work out** – Moving your body is an excellent way to release "steam" and pent-up energy.
- **Count to 100** – Focusing on something else for an extended time helps release the pent-up energy, and turns the focus outward rather than on the problem itself.
- **Breathe in and out, 10 times deeply** – Breathing exercises are among the most POWERFUL ways to calm yourself. Deep calming breaths slow down your heart rate as well as relax tight muscles.
- **Write it down** – Writing things down can help you figure out why you are mad in the first place and how to deal with it. It also brings things into perspective.

---

[30] https://hbr.org/2015/12/calming-your-brain-during-conflict

NOBODY (NOT EVEN YOU) IS PERFECT

We are all flawed individuals, as we all have issues. So be ready to apologize when you screw up. For example, if you said something that caused your friend pain (even if it was not your intention), it's essential to acknowledge what you did. As stated earlier in the book, always confront the person you are having difficulties with, in a private space. Nothing goes far if done in public because the other person will be embarrassed, become defensive, and likely begin to blame you or talk loudly, causing a scene.

THE THING ABOUT APOLOGIZING

You do not want to be a doormat. If you find yourself always apologizing to someone, you need to look at how you are apologizing.

- **If you say, "I'm sorry I said/did that..."** – You are accepting responsibility and saying *what you* did or said was wrong.
- **If you say, "I'm sorry what I said/did made you feel that way..."** – You are accepting your words caused *them* to feel a certain way, which could be a result of their issues.

But seriously, people, apologizing is really one of the best ways to resolve conflict. If you have done something wrong, apologize for it. Don't be proud. Please.

ARE YOU THE PROBLEM?

Do we jump from job to job because of "workplace issues?" If so, we need to take a serious look at our ownership in those situations. Chances are WE may be responsible for many of the conflicts. Other people are NOT always the enemy. We need to own our part in it and of course correct it so we don't repeatedly make the same mistakes.

STOP BEING A HABITUAL HURTER!

If you are habitually hurting people with your words, STOP IT! I suggest you check out Bob Newhart's seven-minute video entitled "Stop It!"[31]

Stop and think before moving ahead in your discussion. When we prepare to have a difficult conversation, we need to ask ourselves some questions:

- Are we triggered? If so, stop.
- What is going on?
- What happened?
- What feelings are we experiencing?
- Did we contribute to the problem?
- Is there a chance we might have misinterpreted what happened?
- Is this a good time to respond, or should we wait?

If we don't manage our triggers (or temper), we will push everyone away from us.

INEFFECTIVE COMMUNICATION

How many times have you heard your colleagues or friends complain that ineffective communication occurs at work or home? It can be frustrating for both parties. And it can lead to a breakdown in the relationship.

---

[31] https://youtu.be/Ow0lr63y4Mw

For example, when there is ineffective workplace communication, the following can result in a lack of trust, fear, insecurity, doubt, silos, competition, shutting down, and withdrawal. The next section will show how this impacts relationships and teams.

DYSFUNCTIONAL TEAMS/RELATIONSHIPS

Without effective communication, it can impact the relationships with our partnerships and teams by enabling dysfunction.

When we think of being on a team, we often think of our workplace. But our spouse/partner, family, and community group could also be considered a team, which is precisely why we must learn how to function as part of a team. Some teams work well, but many teams are dysfunctional.

Author Patrick Lencioni writes about the dysfunction and how to overcome it in his book, *The Five Dysfunctions of a Team: A Leadership Fable.*[32] Based on Lencioni's work, I created a table that outlines the various team dysfunctions to quickly identify where you are and what YOU can do to deal with this scenario.

---

[32] Lencioni, Patrick. The Five Dysfunctions of a Team: A Leadership Fable. San Francisco, Jossey-Bass, April 11, 2002.

TEAM DYSFUNCTIONS

Dysfunction	How to Address It
Absence of Trust	
When trust is absent, it results in a lack of vulnerability (and reduced creativity and innovation), as people keep things close to their chest. We do not speak up for fear of being dismissed, laughed at, or that it will never work.	Speak first, set the tone, and demonstrate you trust your team; and when they push you, it's because they care about the team.
Fear of Conflict	
This type of fear creates an artificial harmony. We pretend everything is just peachy by smiling at our colleagues at work and later complaining about them at home.	Mine for conflict and establish a plan to deal with it. Seek to build authentic relationships.
Lack of Commitment	
A lack of commitment fosters ambiguity, as people will not commit to a deadline or promise, leaving others on the team frustrated.	Encourage clarity to open issues such as commitments. Create closure on issues that have already been resolved.
Avoidance of Accountability	
We do only the minimum, resulting in low standards, impacting the overall company milestones.	Confront difficult issues. Encourage open communication, create clear roles and responsibilities, and use project management systems such as Asana.
Inattention to Results	
We are more concerned with status and ego. We become defensive, and nothing gets resolved.	Encourage and support collective outcomes. Work to overcome individual egos by encouraging teamwork.

Figure 11. Douma, Y. (2021). *Reframe: How to Change Your Conversations to Resolve Those Messy Conflicts*.

IS THE RELATIONSHIP WORTH KEEPING?

As always, some of these tools work, and some do not. That's okay. It is your decision how much time and effort you are going to spend on different relationships. The following scenarios provide you with things to think about:

1. **If it's a boss or colleague,** then you need to get your attitude and outbursts in check real fast, or you may find yourself out of a job! Assess whether the other person is stressed about a work project or personal family matter, and extend some grace.
2. **If it's a close family member** whom you love deeply, it is worth it for you to work it out.
3. **If it's a close friend or partner**, ask yourself what they mean to you. If the relationship is gone from your life, what will it do to you?
4. **If it's a nosy neighbour or community volunteer**, you need to ask how much this relationship (and your reputation) means to you. Because if you have a habit of being rude, it will get around.

MINI-DISCLAIMER:

As I am not a mental health professional or counsellor, I cannot recommend who you have relationships with. I encourage you to choose to keep relationships with people who are supportive and loving. But as always, certain relationships will work for you or not work for you. It is up to YOU to decide who you keep in your life. I'm merely providing you with the tools and questions to evaluate what you need and want for improving your relationships and the quality of your life. If you are in an abusive relationship, or dealing with an acute crisis situation, I highly recommend you immediately seek professional help.

"Every good relationship, especially marriage, is based on respect. If it's not based on respect, nothing that appears to be good will last very long."

– Amy Grant

IN CONCLUSION

From body language, speaking in "I" statements, to active listening and speaking with intention, this chapter provides you with various tools and techniques to communicate.

Whether you are trying to get along with people in the workplace or at home, knowing how to communicate and steer clear of negative conflict effectively will help you build positive relationships.

In the next chapter, I will provide you with various scenarios and case studies to think about how you can apply what you learned in the book if you were in a similar situation.

REFRAME WHAT YOU NOW KNOW

Do you expect people to read your mind, or do you often speak to others when your emotions are all over the place? If so, you need to start learning the techniques taught in this chapter to communicate effectively.

After reading this chapter, you should know how to calm yourself down, maintain boundaries in your relationships, and fess up when you screw up.

Can you see the benefit of pausing to reflect before responding, as outlined in the S-TLC model?

Do you see yourself using the six-step confrontation process as an alternative to the technique I shared in Chapter five (difficult conversations)?

This chapter is full of tools you can implement today!

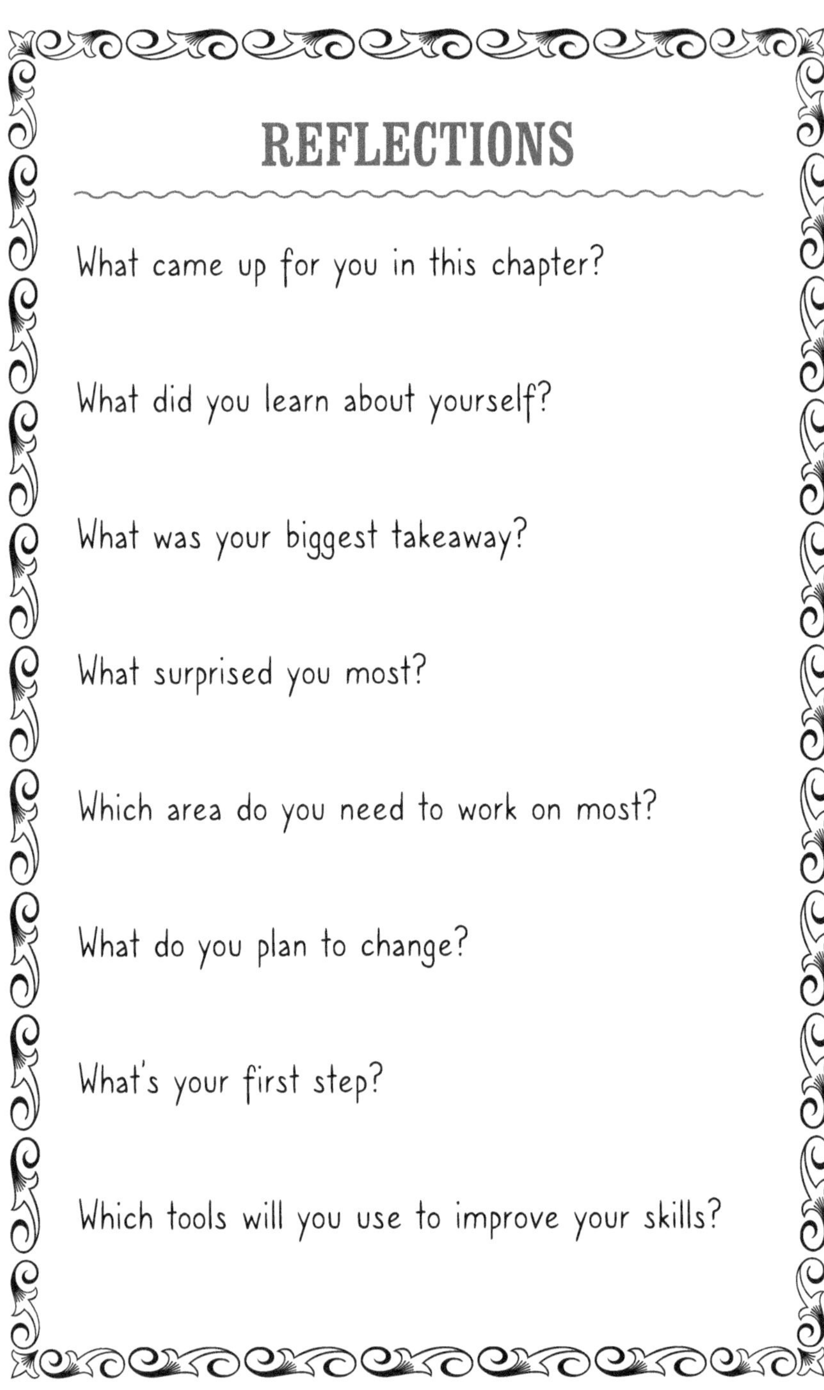

REFLECTIONS

What came up for you in this chapter?

What did you learn about yourself?

What was your biggest takeaway?

What surprised you most?

Which area do you need to work on most?

What do you plan to change?

What's your first step?

Which tools will you use to improve your skills?

CHAPTER NINE

CONFLICT CASE STUDIES

"Conflict is the beginning of consciousness."

– M. Esther Harding

In this chapter, we will be reviewing some scenarios involving conflict so you can identify where your discussions typically fall apart, and what you could have said differently by reframing the communication to change the outcomes.

How do you recognize if you are experiencing difficult conversations? Well, most of us do at some point. As people are complex thinking and feeling beings, it only makes sense that we find ourselves in messy situations that require careful consideration of how we can resolve the problem. Do any of these situations sound familiar to you? If so, you need to learn how to navigate through conflict.

I have provided scenarios relating to the workplace, at home, and in public so you can recognize how your response to these scenarios would be.

To have better outcomes, you need to be motivated to own your part of the problem and solution. We go into this more in Chapter four.

But first, we will look at Maslow's hierarchy of needs, which demonstrates how crucial effective communication is.

NECESSARY FOR HUMAN SURVIVAL AND GROWTH

In 1943, Abraham Maslow introduced his concept of a hierarchy of needs in his published paper entitled "A Theory of Human Motivation." Maslow suggests people are motivated to fulfil their basic needs, as outlined on the pyramid below, before moving on to more advanced needs.

As you will see, with each level, to survive and grow, communication is required. At a fundamental level, we need to communicate our wants and needs to other people. From the bottom of the pyramid moving up, I have listed how communication relates to Maslow's hierarchy of needs:[33]

- **Self-actualization** – Communicate what we want and need, to be empowered and realize our dreams and destiny.
- **Esteem** – Communicate what we want and need, to grow our self-esteem.
- **Love and belonging** – Communicate what we want and need, to foster relationships.
- **Safety** – Communicate what we want and need, to be safe.
- **Physiological needs** – Communicate what we want and need, to live.

---

[33] https://www.simplypsychology.org/maslow.html

Maslow's Hierarchy of Needs

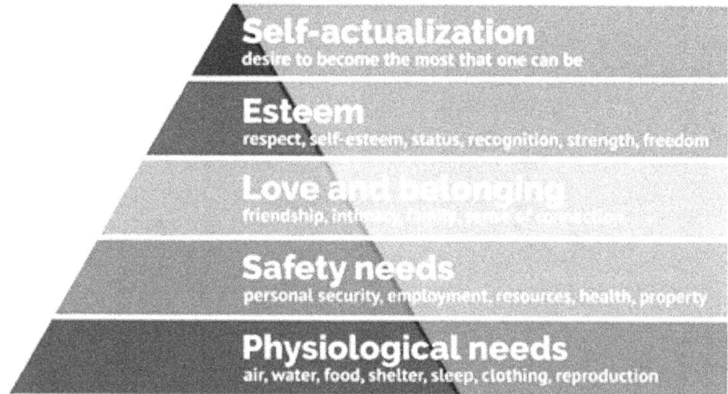

Figure 12. Maslow, A. (1954). Motivation and Personality. Reprinted and retrieved from https://www.simplypsychology.org/maslow.html. Copyright 1954, 1962 by Maslow.

As we see from the above chart, we all have needs. Our needs are not right or wrong; they just are. Understanding your needs is extremely important to recognize the reason you might be feeling down, depressed, anxious, etc. This is also part of emotional intelligence and the Birkman Method. The Birkman Method, in particular, helps identify your needs. Once we understand our needs, we can work towards having those needs nurtured.

Looking at the above chart, do you see any needs you are missing from your life? Is there a way to get these needs met? I would be happy to help you assess your needs and develop solutions that work for you using the Birkman Method. My contact information is listed in the last chapter in this book.

WORKPLACE #1

Description	Workplace: Lazy or Incompetent Administrative Assistant (Admin)
Background	A New boss inherited an assistant who has been with the company for 30 years. The admin is stuck in her ways. She is not tech-savvy and often does things manually (makes lists by hand instead of in Excel or Word). They have a big project coming up, so the new boss needs all employees to work at their best. This is no time for inefficiencies.
Scenario	The boss assigned a project to the admin to prepare a marketing report. The admin did not say she did not have the data already entered into Microsoft Excel. She just nodded and walked away. After checking in with the admin two days later, the admin handed her a 20-page handwritten list of companies on the progress of the report. The boss was understandably shocked by the incompetence.
Dialogue	Boss: I'm not sure what I'm looking at, as I asked for a report. This is handwritten. Why didn't you pull up the data in Excel and run a report? Admin: I don't have any data in Excel. I don't use Excel. This is how I always do it. Boss: Wow, okay. We are a global company and we need to be able to look at data and easily create reports to make decisions that are profitable and sustainable for our company. This is not a junior high school project. I expect you to work with our company standards. This is a busy time for us, so I need you to pull your weight. Admin: Well, I never had to do it this way before. This is how I do it. I don't know what you expect from me. No one ever complained previously. Boss: I expect you to do your job. Or I'll get someone else to do it.

Solution	**How could this have gone differently?** Upon receiving the 20-page handwritten report, the boss could have said, "Let's sit down to discuss this later today. What time works for you?" During the meeting, the boss could say, "Obviously, we have a problem here. How do you think we can work together? I realize you've worked this way for 30 years. But I need you to recognize our data must be entered into the computer. Admin could have responded with, "I'm sorry, I didn't think it would be a problem since it's never been a problem in the past. There is a lot of data to enter. I want to help you with this, but it may take me a while to learn how to use Excel. Is there any way we could pull in an admin from another department to teach me how to do it and assist with the data entry? Going forward, I will be 100% responsible for it. The boss would be pleased the admin took ownership and recognized the urgency of the situation. She also presented a solution, which provides for greater buy-in. The boss's response could be, "Absolutely, we can make that happen. I appreciate you taking ownership of the situation, being open to growing your skillset, and offering a solution that works for both of us. I will look into getting you some help ASAP. There's nothing more I like than team players!"

Figure 13. Douma, Y. (2021). *Reframe: How to Change Your Conversations to Resolve Those Messy Conflicts.*

WORKPLACE #2

<table>
<tr><td>Description</td><td>Workplace: Operations Manager (Ops Mgr.)
Challenging CEO's Authority</td></tr>
<tr><td>Background</td><td>A female Operations Manager was working for a non-profit in a high-profile role. She does visionary work, major fund development, works closely with the Board, and continuously brings in new opportunities. She often receives praise from colleagues and leaders in the organization. But she is feeling bitter, as she knows her bonus will only be 10% of what her female boss (the Executive Director and CEO) will get.</td></tr>
<tr><td>Scenario</td><td>During a company celebratory event, she approaches her boss with her issues, someone she has grown close to over the past ten years and considers a friend.</td></tr>
<tr><td>Dialogue</td><td>
<table>
<tr><td>Ops Mgr.:</td><td>I'm just as valuable as you are.</td></tr>
<tr><td>Boss:</td><td>Well, of course, you are. We are all valuable and worthwhile.</td></tr>
<tr><td>Ops Mgr.:</td><td>No. What I'm saying is I'm worth just as much as you. I know what the senior leadership receives in bonuses, and I think I should get the same percentage. I don't think it's fair I get only 10% of what you get, when I'm the one doing all the work and bringing in all of the revenue.</td></tr>
<tr><td>Boss:</td><td>Look, we all have our place on the org chart. We have a hierarchy for a reason.</td></tr>
<tr><td>Ops Mgr.:</td><td>So you're saying my work isn't valued as much as your work? Therefore, I'm not valued as much as you? Maybe I should go somewhere that appreciates my work.</td></tr>
<tr><td>Boss:</td><td>If that's how you feel.</td></tr>
</table>
</td></tr>
</table>

Solution	**How could this have gone differently:** Being caught off guard, the boss could have acknowledged the feelings of the Ops Mgr by mirroring back what she heard her say. As she values her relationship, she could have suggested they take the conversation offline. During a private conversation, away from work, the boss could have asked what prompted the situation. She could have asked her friend and colleague, "What's going on?" The boss responded defensively, as she felt her identity and authority had been attacked. Instead, she could listen to her colleague with empathy and try to help her get to the bottom of what's going on. Although there may not be a way to change the bonus structure, the boss is in the position to perhaps assist her colleague in another way that makes her feel recognized, valued, and rewarded.

Figure 14. Douma, Y. (2021). *Reframe: How to Change Your Conversations to Resolve Those Messy Conflicts.*

WORKPLACE #3

Description	Workplace Bullying
Background	A new middle manager of a small company, joins a team of wedding planners who will be reporting to her. The team has worked closely together for years and has a natural rhythm to their workflow. They don't adapt nicely to others coming in and trying to change things. They also don't appreciate that one of them wasn't offered the promotion.
Scenario	The new manager was working at her desk when she heard the "ladies" talking negatively about her. She listened for a while and figured they probably needed to blow off steam since one of them was bypassed for her job. The situation escalates, and the negative talk continues throughout the week. Not wanting to step on toes and get her direct reports more upset than they already are, she thought to call them in to meet with her one-on-one. The dialogue is an example of how the conversation went with one of the wedding planners.
Dialogue	

Boss:	I wanted to meet with you to get to know you better. I also wanted to discuss something that has been causing me concern.
Staff:	Really? Did I do something wrong?
Boss:	Actually, yes. I've heard you speaking with the other ladies about me negatively, and I want it to stop.
Staff:	I don't know what you are talking about.
Boss:	I can hear you when my door is open. I'm not stupid. You need to stop this now, or I will write you up in your personnel file for bullying.
Staff:	Bullying? How can I bully you? Last I checked, you are my boss, right? And I don't appreciate being referred to as "ladies" in the workplace.
Boss:	I suggest you read the anti-harassment policies, which include bullying. It does not specify who the recipients of bullying are.
Staff:	Alright. Are we done? Can I go?

Solution	Knowing the wedding planners were upset and resentful the company hired someone externally for the position, she could have set a less combative tone. The new boss should have acknowledged the problematic situation. Stressing how much she values their experience and talent would make them feel appreciated—as well as letting them know she doesn't plan to make their lives more difficult. Instead, she is there to support them. The boss could say, "I've reviewed your performance reviews and of your teammates, and I know how talented you all are. I am grateful for the opportunity to support you with whatever you need. This includes having the opportunity to attend career development training, which will set you up for success and prepare you for future promotions or other career opportunities comingup." To address the negative talk in a less combative way, the boss could have said, "I know how stressful your job can be and how we sometimes need to blow off steam by talking about other people. But I wanted to remind you about our anti-harassment policy, which includes bullying and excessive gossip. As I want to create a positive, supportive culture for our team, I would appreciate you making a conscious effort to please stop gossiping at work. If you are stressed and need support about anything, I have an open-door policy and am here to help you find positive solutions. I truly look forward to working with you, and I thank you for stopping by to meet me. Why don't we set up another meeting to discuss your career goals? We could do it in two weeks, which will give you some time to think about it. How does that sound?"

Figure 15. Douma, Y. (2021). *Reframe: How to Change Your Conversations to Resolve Those Messy Conflicts.*

WORKPLACE #4

Description	Workplace: Board Meeting
Background	A middle-aged woman working as a sales director in a global corporation, for the past 20 years, has always maintained positive relationships with businessmen and has had several male mentors throughout her career. However, there is a new sales manager whose aggressive language has been making her uncomfortable. She's been waiting for the VP of sales to call him on the aggressiveness, but since this new guy has joined the company, it seems as if the "boys' club" is alive and well.
Scenario	The businesswoman presents her plan to the executive team. She invited the new sales manager to the meeting, as he would be responsible for implementing the program. He criticizes her in front of everyone and begins to "mansplain" how sales should be conducted. Mansplaining occurs when a man speaks to a woman in a way that is condescending or patronizing. Aside from the fact he reports to her, he appeared to attack her competency to make himself seem more intelligent. Although their company has a code of conduct, which he violated, no one came to her defence. She is feeling humiliated, dismissed, and extremely upset. She is the only female present, surrounded in the board room by 12 men. She is very defensive and blows up at him in front of everyone.
Dialogue	Woman: "I can't believe you criticized me in front of the executive team. How dare you." Man: "What are you talking about? I was only voicing my concern on a few elements of your presentation. They just didn't make sense." Woman: "I don't care. You humiliated me, and that is your second warning. Strike three, and you are out." Man: "I don't get this. I am supposed to be the manager here. When I am looking out for the company, you get ticked off. I don't get it."

Dialogue	Woman: "You're kidding me, right? You won't even acknowledge you went over the line?" Man: "No, I won't." Woman: "You're suspended without pay for a week. I will see how I feel after you come back."
Solution	**How could this have gone differently?** To understand a bit better, the boss was feeling insecure and threatened by her manager. She felt he was throwing her under the bus. She was angry and wanted to scream. Instead, if she had managed to calm down before the meeting with the manager, she would have been more in charge. She needed to stop and think, and question what really happened in the meeting. Did her manager throw her under the bus? Did he intend to belittle her? Why would he do this? What would his purpose be for doing this? They have had a good working relationship in the past, and this incident was out of character for him. What had happened had affected her identity. She thought the presentation was terrific, and it was an excellent plan for future growth. It was. Her manager made a few comments, but was his intention to hurt her? She could have proceeded with having a difficult conversation, asking him to go for coffee, and saying she was uncomfortable with the way the meeting went. At coffee, she could have told him she felt sabotaged, and ask if this was his intent. Allowing him an opportunity to explain himself, she may have discovered he wasn't trying to sabotage her, and he was indeed adding value to the plan that was already excellent. To prevent this from happening again, she could have asked him to relay his concerns about presentations, in detail, before it is due. They could have deepened their working relationship and become an even better team.

Solution	This may not necessarily turn out the way I have suggested above; however, at least the boss would feel more in control. She could get a better sense of the manager and what his skills were. Perhaps she could include him earlier in the process of planning the presentation. After all, he was the manager. Either trust will develop or she will identify whether or not he is a good fit for the business. On top of it all, she will be more confident and sure of future decisions.

Figure 16. Douma, Y. (2021). *Reframe: How to Change Your Conversations to Resolve Those Messy Conflicts*.

FAMILY/HOME #1

Description	Home: Married Couple
Background	The wife is the breadwinner, and the husband is the stay-at-home parent. She is driven and tends to work late, which upsets her husband. He loves her and wants to spend time with her and their two-year-old daughter. He also is very supportive of her career ambition.
Scenario	The wife gets home late from work without calling her husband to give him a heads up. She's tired and stressed out and just wants to have a shower and go to bed. She had a late lunch, so she's not very hungry. He has prepared a nice dinner for them, which got cold. He is frustrated, and he blows up at her not long after she walks through the door.
Dialogue	Husband: I'm so sick and tired of you coming home late all the time. I cooked for an hour and a half. And you're not even eating my dinner. You didn't even say thank you. Wife: Do you need to give me a kiss or a hug the second I come through the door? You were pretty quick to attack me.

<table>
<tr><td>Dialogue</td><td><table><tr><td>Wife:</td><td>Are you kidding me? I just worked 10 hours today. I'm exhausted. I got this new boss breathing down my neck, and my colleagues have a knife in my back with every move I make.</td></tr><tr><td>Husband:</td><td>You don't think raising a baby is stressful?</td></tr></table></td></tr>
<tr><td>Solution</td><td>How could this have gone differently?

The husband could have texted his wife and said, "Hun, I'd love to make a special dinner for us tonight. What time do you think you're going to get home?"

Knowing she'd have to work late, she could have responded with, "Babe, tonight is not the best night. I appreciate your thought. You're so good to me. I could use some "we time," so could we schedule it for a night when I know I'll be able to leave work by 6 p.m.?

In this scenario, both the husband and wife feel valued and respected.</td></tr>
</table>

Figure 17. Douma, Y. (2021). *Reframe: How to Change Your Conversations to Resolve Those Messy Conflicts.*

FAMILY/HOME #2

Description	Messy Adult Children Who Come to Visit
Background	Grandparents have great relationships with their adult children and grandchildren. They enjoy spending time with them and are grateful for every second they are together.
Scenario	They recently had a beautiful above-ground pool installed in their huge backyard. Their adult children and grandkids come over every weekend to enjoy the pool and backyard. But while they are there, they leave behind a huge mess. The grandmother is upset but doesn't want to make a big deal of it. But she's also sick and tired of cleaning up after her adult kids! She has an *inner* conflict brewing inside her for weeks before she finally gets the nerve to confront her kids. This demonstrates her internal dialogue as she goes back and forth on whether or not to confront them.
Dialogue	

Mom:	Okay, I'm going to have to say something. I'm tired of doing dishes, putting away food, picking up wet towels, and putting pool toys into the bin. I shouldn't have to clean up after them!
Mom:	But I don't want to upset them. I love spending time with them. I don't want them to feel bad either. I know they work hard, and taking care of the kids is not easy. I'm sure they don't mean to be inconsiderate.
Mom:	Yes, but this is ridiculous! I'm not their maid!
Mom:	Wait, am I overreacting? I know how particular I can be with having a clean house.
Mom:	Maybe I shouldn't say anything. I'll just clean up afterwards.

Solution	This type of inner discussion had been going on for far too long. The grandmother could have said, "You know how much your dad and I love spending time with you. But we are getting too old to be picking up after you. Could you please spend some time cleaning up so it looks the same when you leave as it did when you arrived?"

Figure 18. Douma, Y. (2021). *Reframe: How to Change Your Conversations to Resolve Those Messy Conflicts.*

"Whenever you're in conflict with someone, there is one factor that can make the difference between damaging your relationship and deepening it. That factor is attitude."

– William James

IN CONCLUSION

This chapter features case studies you can relate to, including examples in the workplace and at home. As you can see, there are many ways to respond and react, but there are fewer ways that are effective. Becoming emotional and freaking out quickly escalates a manageable conflict into one that is dysfunctional and at times downright abusive. Getting sucked into the vortex of generalizations, and getting defensive when being confronted in a public forum, are also recipes for disaster.

Therefore, your first line of defence is to put some distance and allow time for you to think about what was said to you and how it made you feel.

REFRAME
WHAT YOU NOW KNOW

You learned how to diffuse the situation by simply saying, "I'm sorry you feel that way. I'm not in a position to talk about it right now. I don't want to overreact. And I don't want to say something that might hurt us."

You can see how this type of response makes them feel heard and can calm them down.

I'm sure by now you realize the importance of scheduling a time for the two of you to meet offsite. The scheduled appointment allows you both time to think about what you want to say—and more importantly, learn about their perspective. And when you meet and listen to their story (before responding), you are much more likely to come to an amicable solution.

REFLECTIONS

What came up for you in this chapter?

What did you learn about yourself?

What was your biggest takeaway?

What surprised you most?

Which area do you need to work on most?

What do you plan to change?

What's your first step?

Which tools will you use to improve your skills?

CHAPTER TEN

FINAL THOUGHTS

"Conflict is drama, and how people deal with conflict shows you the kind of people they are."

– Steven Moyer

You have almost made it to the end of the book! I commend you on wanting to improve your communication and conflict management skills. This chapter will provide you with a quick overview of the chapters we have covered. It will also offer some of the key concepts, techniques, and tips that are easy to implement so you can feel more confident when communicating with others.

MY PURPOSE

As I shared with you in my introduction, my intention for writing this book was to create a tool that could help you communicate effectively. More specifically, I wanted to teach you how to change your conversations in the workplace and everyday relationships to resolve those messy conflicts in your life.

I hope after reading this book, you will know how to avoid

triggers that typically set you off and put you on the path of being stuck in unhealthy, self-destructive relationships.

By avoiding triggers, you will have peace and harmony in your life—instead of conflict and chaos—thus providing you with a greater sense of safety. You will feel confident navigating difficult conversations with ease, resulting in improvements in your productivity, focus, and leadership abilities.

****By no means is this book inclusive of dealing with all conflict situations or deep, serious conflicts. It is to be used as a tool—or guide—to help you make the best of your relationships. It is not to diagnose illnesses that need to be treated by medical practitioners.** **

RECAP OF THE BOOK CHAPTERS

I wanted us to revisit what we've covered in the previous nine chapters.

- **Chapter one:** We looked at conflict. Why it happens, what our part is, and how our past trauma and current triggers impact our ability to effectively communicate, all come into play when it comes to healthy communication and conflict.
- **Chapter two:** We looked at emotional intelligence (self-awareness, self-management, social awareness, and relationship management.) Understanding and knowing ourselves is critical for relating to others and having positive, healthy relationships.
- **Chapter three:** We saw the effects our limiting beliefs and stress have on our everyday lives. We learned about our brain's stress response and evaluated how we respond in stressful workplace situations.

- **Chapter four:** This chapter was all about our communication styles and our responses. I provided examples of dysfunctional responses, and proposed functional responses to see how different communication methods have a direct correlation to the success of our relationships.
- **Chapter five:** I prepared you for having a difficult conversation—a critical skill to know how to resolve conflict effectively.
- **Chapter six:** We looked at passive-aggression. I included a diagnostic tool and tips on how to overcome passive-aggression (if you are the problem) and how to confront the behaviour of others.
- **Chapter seven:** This chapter was all about dealing with angry people. I have provided tools on how to diffuse the situation and recognize when to call it quits in the case of abusive, toxic people that are causing you harm (when you have exhausted all other strategies).
- **Chapter eight:** I provided you with a range of quick tips for maintaining positive relationships. Everything from body language, tone, to specific words was covered.
- **Chapter nine:** I provided you with various case studies about dealing with conflict at work, home, and in public spaces. I hope you will apply the tools and strategies you have learned throughout the book, should you find yourself in similar situations.

COMMUNICATION IS A FUNDAMENTAL SKILL SET

If you haven't noticed already, I am very passionate about communication. I mean, how can I not love it? Communication is so powerful, and it's a necessary part of everyday life.

We all need to communicate to function and get along with others. Yet, shockingly, this essential skill is not taught in schools.

Consequently, we grow up learning language and communication skills from our parents, peers, and teachers. We also hear it in the media, which are not the best role models. What we realize is some people are terrible communicators! They use their words as missiles, to hurt and cause harm to others. Sometimes, it's not intentional. And then there are others with passive-aggressive and aggressive/angry tendencies who do it on purpose. Regardless of the intention, communication is a skill that can be learned. Our words should not cause others harm!

Then some people hide in their shells and don't stand up for themselves during confrontations. They suffer in silence because they don't have the confidence or skills to articulate what they want or need. Bottling up negative feelings and emotions can cause harm to us. So they must learn how to have difficult conversations.

The goal with communication, and more specifically conflict, is to have a happy medium whereby both parties have a win-win.

I truly believe communication should be taught in elementary and high schools, as communication is a fundamental skill we all require. When we grow up lacking these skills, it can have a detrimental effect on our lives. We could experience problems with keeping a job or maintaining relationships. Without a solid support system, we could self-destruct.

As it takes two to tango, it's necessary for us to look at what we bring to the table. Are we communicating effectively? Let's check out this self-assessment tool and implement the tips to stay calm during a conflict.

ARE YOU THE PROBLEM? THE IMPORTANCE OF SELF-ASSESSMENT

When workplace or personal relationships have many conflicts, there is a good chance *you* may be part of the problem. Just as it takes two people to make a relationship work, it takes two to break it. In other words, if you are not contributing to the success of your relationships, you may very well be contaminating them.

There are many different self-assessment models that can be used, including the Birkman Method mentioned in Chapter two. However, I have provided you with some questions to help gauge if you could be causing the communication problems. Think about some of the previous workplace conflicts that occurred, where there was some communication breakdown or a blow-up where things got heated.

QUESTIONS TO HELP DETERMINE IF YOU ARE THE PROBLEM

1. What was the problem or issue?
2. Were there previous issues with that person?
3. What were your emotions? Were you angry or frustrated?
4. Have previous workplace conflicts like this caused you pain or embarrassment? Be honest with yourself.
5. Are you harbouring any open wounds or resentments towards someone at work?
6. What was your role in the situation? Are you willing to own your part in what happened?
7. What choices (or behaviour) did you make if you would do differently if given the opportunity?
8. How do your colleagues or boss typically treat you?

9. Does the situation or relationship require a difficult conversation? If so, go back to Chapter five and prepare to have the conversation so you can come to a resolution and restore peace in your working relationship.

"Peace is not absence of conflict, it is the ability to handle conflict by peaceful means."

– Ronald Reagan

IN CONCLUSION

This concludes our discussion of changing our conversations to resolve messy conflicts. I wanted to provide you with some quick tips you could implement today to improve your relationships. Let me end with a few thoughts.

Conflict is not easy. Because we know conflict causes stress, and stress causes physical health problems, and because physical health problems can land you in a hospital bed, would you agree it's pretty essential you address any issues you are experiencing?

Doing conflict well is hard. You will not conquer doing healthy conflict in one day. If you have been living in conflict for years, it will take a lot of training to undo the way you have been doing conflict. I understand that communicating how we feel and the impact someone else's actions have on us is one of the hardest things people face.

So please, let me emphasize. This book is not a guarantee you will resolve conflict in a healthy way. I hope it gave you some insight into the work you will have to deal with healthy conflict.

Many people have mind-body practices to release anger and hurt, such as going to yoga to relax and stretch (and especially hot yoga to sweat out stress). Others go to their family doctor or therapist. Whatever you need, seek it out so you can remain healthy.

What I don't want to happen for you is to read this book and ignore the information and say it's "just fluff."

I can assure you, based on all the research done on conflict, including my own experiences in my life and of my clients, the information in this book is real. It is a compilation of over 20 years of leadership experience, research during my studies for my Master of Arts in Leadership, reading hundreds of books, teaching in the undergrad Leadership program, helping my clients, and living in conflict in my own life. I can't make this stuff up.

Change does not come easy. Your brain has been infiltrated with how you have been doing things for years. I see some of my clients move from job to job or relationship to relationship, thinking the grass will be greener on the other side. What they tend to forget is wherever they go, they will be taking themselves with them. If nothing changes with them, nothing changes.

So the question is…

Are you ready to change your life?

If you read this book and took the opportunities to assess what's happening for you, then you have learned a TON. I believe you are ready—even if you don't believe it.

REFRAME WHAT YOU NOW KNOW

Here is what you have learned from reading this book:

- Changing your communication style can change a toxic workplace.
- The way you communicate can help others understand you better.
- Your role on the team changes with you.
- Difficult conversations do not need to be difficult.
- You can save relationships by listening with the intent to understand.

When things have been festering for a while, you will need to deal with it as soon as possible, as you will either blow up one day or stuff down unhealthy feelings and emotions. In workplaces, the negative energy you may be holding onto often seeps into the environment, creating a toxic work environment for your team.

By listening and engaging with a person, you can change how you react to people you are in conflict with instead of avoiding. I'm talking about your reaction, not the reaction of others.

Once you communicate effectively to others about how their behaviour affects you, you will likely notice 98% of your conflicts are about misunderstandings.

Therefore, make a plan to deal with the problem. Your workplace relationships will improve by being willing to listen and really hear the other person's story and then go on to share yours!

Moreover, when other people in your work start seeing you do this, they start saying, "Wow! She is so powerful. She dealt with that beautifully." You will gain immense respect from the rest of the team and create a ripple effect as others will start to behave the same way as you! You will become a role model for effective communication and leadership.

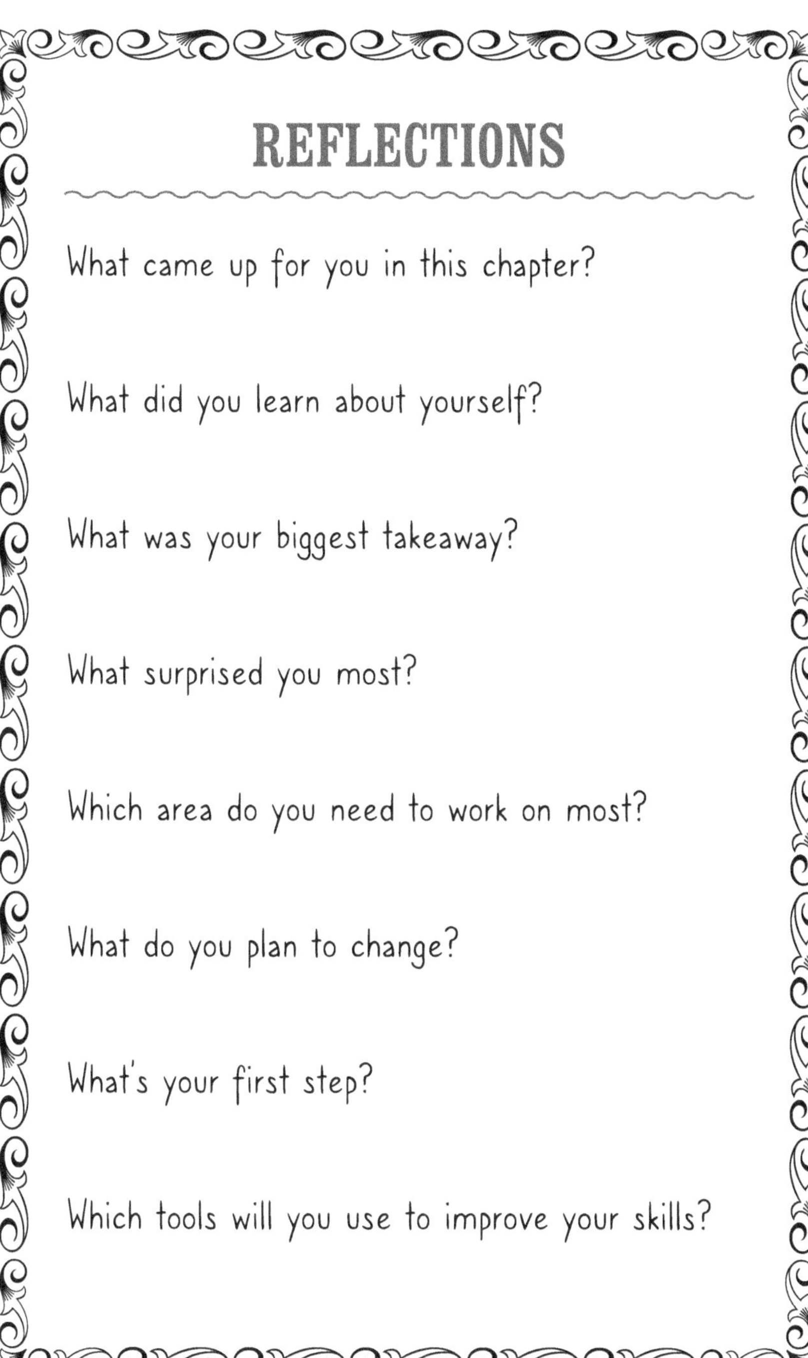

REFLECTIONS

What came up for you in this chapter?

What did you learn about yourself?

What was your biggest takeaway?

What surprised you most?

Which area do you need to work on most?

What do you plan to change?

What's your first step?

Which tools will you use to improve your skills?

IF YOU WANT TO LEARN MORE

The information provided in this book is an introduction to this subject matter.

If any of this resonated with you, or if you would like to talk through a specific conflict, I am happy to offer a 15-minute free discovery call to discuss a situation you are currently dealing with.

If you are interested in group coaching, join me in "Winning the Workplace Power Struggle as a Female Leader." This can be found at www.doumaleadership.ca.

The benefits of working with me in my coaching program include:

- Feeling empowered and confident
- Having more energy and motivation to pursue dreams and goals
- Feeling better (physically and mentally)
- Having the courage to stand up to bullies, and angry and passive-aggressive people
- Having the confidence to bust through the ceilings

- Building your career and make the income you deserve
- Having less stress at work and in life
- No longer feeling like an imposter
- Having no more doubts and fears
- Having stronger time management skills
- Having excellent family and work relationships
- Having more excitement and fun in all aspects of your life

You can also visit my websites, to download some additional bonuses, including:

- Free download – 45-minute Masterclass on Difficult Conversations and Worksheet (value $249) at www.YvonneDouma.com
- Free 15-minute discovery call (value $100) at www.DoumaLeadership.ca

www.ingramcontent.com/pod-product-compliance
Lightning Source LLC
LaVergne TN
LVHW050639100826
845148LV00011B/1911